Mountain Bike Guide

San Diego Region

By
Scott Bringe

Sunbelt Publications, Inc.
San Diego

Sunbelt Publications, Inc.
POB 191126
San Diego, CA 92159-1126.

Library of Congress Cataloging-in-Publication Data

Bringe, Scott, 1964-
  Mountain bike guide - San Diego region / by Scott Bringe. -
- 3rd Rev. ed.
    p.   cm.
  Includes bibliographical references and index.
  ISBN 0-932653-19-7: $11.95
  1. All terrain cycling--California--San Diego County--Guide-books.
2. Bicycle touring--California--San Diego County--Guide-books. 4 San
Diego County (Calif.)--Description and travel--Guide-books.
I. Title.
GV1045.5.C22S253 1993
796.6'4'0979498--dc20   90-40002
                                                  CIP

1 2 3 4 5 6 7 8 9 10

To

The great out-of-doors and those who love it;

may we never lack for either.

Acknowledgments

Many people contributed to the preparation of this book; so many that I cannot hope to recognize each one. But I particularly want to acknowledge:

● Jim Vrakas for checking the accuracy of the trail descriptions, transit times, and trail configurations.

● Bob Nelson of the San Diego Parks and Recreation Department for data provided.

● Lowell Lindsay for new photographs, editing of this edition, and natural history notes.

● Marian Bringe for her development of maps and contributions to text.

● Dan Bradley for computer support.

● Jon Lindsay for providing the illustrations, cover, and additional field testing.

● Bill Hample for the design and initial editing of this book.

● The Lindsays of Sunbelt Publications and Able Printing, who have published and printed the several editions of this book.

● And finally the trail explorers, riding companions, bike store operators and a host of other San Diegans who, over the years, have contributed to the biking experiences I have described in this book.

Photo Credits

Photo credits as noted in captions:

BH	Bill Hample	LL	Lowell Lindsay
CDP	Calif. Dept. Parks & Recreation	NS	Nancy Smith
DEL	Diana Lindsay	SB	Scott Bringe

I thank you all.

Scott Bringe
Scottsdale, Arizona
September 1993

Contents

CUYAMACA STATE PARK features many miles of dirt road for mountain bikers and other non-motorized recreationists. - DEL

Part I

Introduction

Preface

Welcome to mountain bike routes in the San Diego County region! Seven hundred miles of routes open to mountain bicyclists are spread throughout the 25 tour areas, featuring 55 trips, included herein. Our county has over one third of her land dedicated to public use. Pedal only blocks from downtown and you find trails at bays, beaches, and in tree-shrouded canyons. Few have recognized the impressive network of bicycle trails we have here. Mountain bikes, however, are changing that "few" to "many."

Since *Mountain Bike Trail Guide - San Diego Edition* first appeared in 1988, the popularity of mountain biking in San Diego County and in the nation has rapidly accelerated. Thus, much of the data given in the 1988 first edition required updating and a revised second edition was published in 1990. For similar reasons, the book is again being revised in this, the 1993 third editon. Some progress has been made in relations between cyclists, hikers and horseback riders, although challenges still exist. We hope relations continue to improve.

It is most important that mountain bikers be aware of all laws, rules and regulations pertaining to mountain biking the tour areas described. We have outlined the major points in the sections which follow. Common courtesy and consideration for the rights of others, and for the environment, are the simplest and most important.

Not enough can be said about maintaining your bike in good working order. Several of the tours in this book are set in remote, isolated areas where a breakdown could be hazardous. We have included tips on bike care and maintenance which we have found useful in our own experience.

Finally, may this revised edition aid all in pursuing our one common interest - - the enjoyment of San Diego's great out-of-doors.

Scott Bringe
September 1993

A Note On the Right-Of-Way and Biking Safety

Research at the San Diego County Assessor's Office was undertaken to determine the ownership of areas described in the maps and text of this book. Some areas were undefined as to the right-of-way for mountain bicyclists. Others may become fully subject to the enforcement of existing or new laws. The areas described in this book, and included in its maps, were in open use by mountain bicyclists at the time of this publication. Readers are warned, however, that the right to pass over any properties may change at any time without notice.

The author and publisher have taken all reasonable measures to ensure the accuracy of the route descriptions contained herein. Even so, mountain biking entails certain unavoidable risks, and trail conditions may have changed after this book was written. For these reasons, the descriptions in this book are not representations that a particular trip will be safe for you or your party. When you take a trip, you assume responsibility for your own safety. Keeping informed about current trail conditions, weather changes, and the legal right-of-way, combined with common sense, are the keys to a safe, enjoyable tour. Due to the possibilities of injury or legal conflict arising from any errors or false information within this book, the author and publisher assume no liability in connection with its contents.

An ample supply of water (and frequent consumption thereof) is the most important single safety consideration.

Comments and updates are most welcome and should be sent to:

Sunbelt Publications, Inc.
POB 191126
San Diego, CA 92159-1126

Sunbelt Publications, Inc.
San Diego, 1993

Some Legal and Ethical Considerations

Included here are some of the legal postings mountain bikers may meet when traversing the tours of this book. These legalities are usually prominently posted and are mandatory. The following are some of the more common signs you may see.

In the City of San Diego:

**OFF-ROAD
VEHICLE
ACTIVITY
PROHIBITED**

This sign pertains to motorized vehicles.

In the Cleveland National Forest:

**O.R.V.
PROHIBITED**
(Off-Road Vehicles Prohibited)

You will see this sign in certain areas. It means that certain motorized vehicles

are allowed in the area, BUT - they must be highway-legal and they must stay on the existing trails. That goes for mountain bikes too -- stay on the trails.

O.R.V.
AREA
(Off-Road Vehicle Area)

This basically means no route restrictions for motorcycles, mountain bikes, tanks anywhere within the ORV Area borders unless otherwise posted.

In Wilderness Areas:
No wheeled vehicles of any type (mountain bikes included) are allowed in Wilderness Areas.

In Anza-Borrego Desert State Park:
Similar to Cleveland National Forest. All wheeled vehicles must stay on approved, existing vehicle trails. (See Tour No. 20, Coyote Canyon, for a more detailed discussion of state park rules.).

In Los Peñasquitos Canyon Preserve:
Los Peñasquitos Canyon Preserve (Tour No. 3) is probably the most popular and diverse of all the preserved areas in the city. Unfortunately, it is also the first public area in which trail restrictions for mountain cyclists have become an issue. One major factor which has fanned the controversy has been the misuse of the area by careless bike riders. The complaints are not new and are common to many areas. These have included: (1) excessive speeds by bikers which endanger horseback riders and hikers; (2) failure by bikers to yield the right-of-way to all non-bike trail users (mountain bikers have least precedence on the trail and must yield to all others); (3) damage to sensitive vegetation and wildlife habitats by bikers riding cross-country or employing other "banzai" maneuvers; (4) failure by bikers to cross streams at established, low-impact points.

A major factor which will decide whether or not we are banned from Los Peñasquitos Canyon (or any multi-user area) is the support that we give the issue NOW, both at the hearings and, of course, on the trail. Cleaning up our act is something we all must attend to and stay with. Appreciation for the rights of others and of the environment is required from all of us. However, across the nation mountain bikers are losing out as the well-organized forces of equestrians and hikers mobilize votes to squelch the "metal horses." Trying to reopen an area after it has been closed is almost impossible.

Organizations:
One group that is dedicated to the rights and proper decorum of mountain bikers is the Off-Road Cycling Association (ORCA). This group has established a local Land Access Committee providing San Diego County mountain bikers with representation at meetings and hearings on access issues. This group has formulated preventive measures which are crucial to the maintenance of present trail access by bikers and they need the full support of all of us. Our

sudden emergence as users of the out-of-doors, has generated much anti-biker sentiment. To offset these arguments, we need to organize and reach agreements with others. The old saying, "In unity there is strength," most certainly applies to us. We must gain the respect of foot and horseback enthusiasts who are understandably offended by our latter day chrome-moly horses.

Another fine organization working in our behalf is the International Mountain Bike Association (IMBA). Join them. Join ORCA - you will not only help save our trails, you will be able to stay abreast of the latest laws and issues affecting our sport. If we can stay on top of the apathy that has allowed so much ground to slip away in other cities, we can maintain in San Diego County one of the finest trail systems in the country.

For further information contact:

ORCA   IMBA
10507 Caminito Glenellen   Rt. 2, Box 303
San Diego, CA 92126   Bishop, CA 92514

We mountain bikers are newcomers on the trail. Whether areas will remain open to us depends to a large extent on the positive or negative encounters we have with hikers and horses. A good idea when rolling is to alert people as far ahead as possible. Always yield to oncoming traffic, especially equestrians. Stay on the trails. Riding cross-country damages fragile ecosystems and can be dangerous. Finally, wait at least a day after a rain before hitting the trail. Don't leave ruts in mud. They are a pain in the seat and ankle when they harden.

A Word About Bike Mechanics

Simple Maintenance

Clean and oil your chain every time you go out. This will save you money in the long run. The only method I have found which keeps the chain from squeaking after 50 miles of sand, water, etc. is as follows: (1) Clean the chain. A rag will work, but an actual chain cleaner is better for removing grit inside the links and rollers. (2) Spray the chain rollers with a light coat of an oil containing Teflon (there are several popular brands on the market). This light oil works its way into the interior of the chain, but it's not heavy enough to last by itself, when dirt or water get on the chain. (3) To keep the chain quiet, add a second light coat of a heavier oil, such as SAE 30 motor oil. All of this may sound time-consuming, but it's worth it. The Teflon on the inner surfaces of the chain provides excellent lubrication and the heavier oil on the outside will take you that extra mile.

As you ride, the chain will stretch. If this is allowed past a certain point, it will wear out the gears. Once the gear teeth are worn down, the chain will eventually skip. After wear has occurred, a new chain will rumble and try to skip even if skipping hasn't started. This happens because the old chain and gears have worn in together, too far. At that point it may be worthwhile to reinstall the old chain and let it go until it skips. The new chain won't work properly without replacing at least some of the gears. Monitoring your chain stretch and replacing it ($15) in time will triple the life of your freewheel ($30). You may be able to go through 10 chains before you have to replace your front chain rings ($80). This is in comparison to these same costs entailed by using only one skipping chain. My chains last about 300-600 miles. Miles between replacements, however, will depend upon how much low gear torque you put on your chain and how well you lubricate it. A quick, but rough, way to check chain stretch is to place the chain on the large chain ring in front when both are clean and not oiled. Then pull forward on the chain from the front edge of the chain ring. If you can pull the chain off the chain ring 1/4" or more, it has probably been stretched to the maximum. This method is rough because a worn chain ring and/or pulling very hard will add slop to the measurement. When in doubt, replace the chain and if the new chain is quiet, you are in luck. If you think you replaced the chain too soon, you still have the old chain with which you can compare slop measurements.

Gearing

Experts say the bicycle is the most efficient means for moving the body as a machine. Unfortunately, most mountain bikes don't come stock with low enough gearing to enable one to stay on the bike while going up some of the hills that San Diego has to offer. The reason may be that bike manufacturers realize low gears put much more torque on the chain and the rest of the drive train. This leads to the problems previously mentioned. Other problems can develop; example: bottom brackets and crank arms which loosen and burn out because they often go unnoticed until it's too late. It would appear that manufacturers are more concerned with product durability than whether you ride or push your bike up the hill. Currently the lowest gear that is available for the front (small chain ring) in the non-round style is a 26 tooth gear (stock is usually 28). You can go much lower if you want to use round chain rings. This could entail going as low as a 16 tooth gear, added on as a fourth chain ring, but that's a lot of customizing. A 24 tooth round gear replacement of the small, existing chain ring is probably the easiest way to get the needed ratio. The next thing you can do is change the gears on your freewheel (rear). On most bikes that means replacing the whole cluster of gears, and isn't cheap. On more expensive bikes, with cassette freewheels, you can replace individual gears. The lowest you can go in the rear (biggest gear) is a 34 tooth gear (stock is usually 28). I personally run a 32 tooth in the rear and 26 tooth non-round in the front. I find this perfect for the steepest hills on which I can get enough traction to ride to the summit. With any lower gearing you will be going so slow that it becomes difficult to remain balanced. Obtaining new components and better gear ratios may result in even greater limitations.

Tubes and Tires

Replace stock tubes with puncture-resistant tubes. Do not use tire liners alone. Thorns do penetrate liners. Thorns can come in through the tire sides and by-pass liners. Further, as soon as a thorn punctures a regular tube, the tube pops. On the other hand, a thorn may penetrate a thorn-resistant tube, but the tube will still hold air. Days later the tube will still be firm enough to ride on, even with several thorns in it. Do not pull these out on the trail; they are your temporary patches! Puncture-resistant tubes add a pound to the bike, but so do liners. So do seldom-used tools and pumps. Let me put it this way. I haven't been stranded once since I switched to thick tubes five years ago. This, of course, doesn't mean it can't happen. Many factors have an influence on tire life. Some say that tire life is a personal thing. We think they mean that tire life is almost directly proportional to the type of riding to which tires are exposed and the care which they receive. There are tires that are designed with interlocking treads, forming a center ridge which make pavement riding smoother and more efficient. However, these pavement tires don't do as well off-road as the knobbier open-tread patterns. Use wider tires if you plan on doing any riding in sand; use narrow tires if weight is the primary concern.

The more repairs you learn to do yourself, although painful at first, the faster you will become one-with-your-machine. This allows the most fun on the trail, and will save you money in the long run. It's easy to spend much more on repairs than the original cost of the bike.

Sand Riding Technique

Pedaling through sand adds an unpredictable dimension to mountain biking. Almost every trail will have sand on it in some place, and a gew trails will have throughout. Every mountain bicyclist must learn methods of tackling sand. These methods are for marginal sand sections that are almost better walk-the-bike through.

A. Reducing Air Pressure

The easiest technique is simply reducing air pressure in the tires. This works like snowshoes, as it allows the tires to spread out giving more surface.

There are some drawbacks to this method however.

First, you need to let a lot of air out of your tires (down to 10-20 psi., depending on your weight) before they effectively spread out. That may be OK if the whole trip is sand, but it's a real drag to pedal with nearly flat tires if you have alternating sand and hard surfaces. Pumping your tires at the end of sandy stretches can take more time than pushing your bike through the tough spots.

Second, a tire with standard air pressure (35-65 psi.) protects the rims. Therefore, if the sand has rocks here and there, you're risking not only denting a rim, but getting a flat tire as the inner tube becomes pinched between rock, tire, and rim.

Third, if you hit the brakes extremely hard with low tire pressure, the tire may have spin free of the rim taking the inner tube with it. If you're lucky, your valve stem will only be sticking slanted out of the rim hole. If not, the valve stem will get ripped off, and no patch can fix it. Valve stem shearing can actually occur with tire pressures up to 50 psi if you are heavy, headed down a steep, paved hill at a high speed, and you hit the front brake hard. But it's hard to go fast in sand, and usually the last thing you're trying to do is stop!

B. Gearing

Since you're going to be going relatively slow (5 mph) through the thick stuff, shift into the small, left chain ring in front, and 2nd or 3rd gear (from the left) in the rear sprocket BEFORE you enter the sand. (Once in the sand you have to keep pedaling to stay afloat and the last thing you can do is shift.).

Being in this low gear forces you to pedal relatively fast (high rpm) which keeps the rear tire at a constant speed. (Pedaling slow gives the rear tire spurts that force the tire down instead of forward.).

Avoid using your lowest gear in thick sand because you're just going too slow. You need to keep up some speed, otherwise every rotation of the rear tire is going to dig you down rather than push you forward. From a dead-stop it is helpful to start in a higher gear (third lowest or so) and try to get forward momentum with your body just before you quickly get your second foot on the pedals in time to make a smooth spin of the crank.

C. Balance and Tracking

The heavier you are, the harder it's going to be to avoid sinking in sand. One way to ease this sinking problem is to balance your weight between the tires. Do this by shifting your body forward on the bike. This will take practice to perfect.

Probably the most technical thing about riding sand is keeping a steady balance and riding as straight a line as possible. When you turn the front wheel, it slows down the bike because the front tire is no longer rolling over the sand, but plowing it to the side. Therefore, the straighter the line you ride, the easier the riding well be.

Turns have to be done gradually and "planned for." Sharp turns will slow or stop the bike.

D. Cleanup

The last thing about sand is the threat it poses to the mountain bike as a machine. Sand is the ultimate abrasive and finds itself a home in all the exposed oily surfaces of the bike such as chains, gears, and derailleurs.

Be nice to your bike; it can take you miles away from civilization. It can also leave you there.

How To Use This Book

This guide was created to minimize trip planning time and to maximize enjoyable trail time. A grid map accompanies each tour described in the text. Key locations in the text are referenced by their grid coordinates as shown on the respective tour map. Columns are designated by number, rows by letter. Example: referring to the map for Tour No. 1, the parking area at Torrey Pines State Park mentioned in the text is referenced by its grid coordinates (G, 4). That is, this parking area is located at the intersection of Row 'G' and Column '4'. Note on the map that a parking symbol, "P", is also shown at this grid point. A system of symbols has been developed and is common to all maps. See the "Map Key", referenced in the Table of Contents, for symbol definitions and other information.

In the text, an overview of the tour area is given for each tour. Most of the tours have been divided into sub-tours or trips. The length of the trip in miles and estimated time to complete the trip are given. The most desirable season in which to make the trip is stated. All trips are rated in terms of general difficulty by one to five stars, with one being easy. Example: one star might represent areas with wide, flat trails; five stars might describe severe areas which require dismounting to pass. A description of the trail surface is given for each trip; its climb/descent range in elevation, and average elevation change per mile are stated. Route directions for arriving at the tour area by auto are given, along with descriptions of the trail itself, as the bike tour progresses.

Many books have been written describing the proper gear and clothing mountain bikers should wear and we see no need to duplicate this information. Climate and weather, however, have much to do with tour enjoyment. To aid in deciding what you will wear or take along, we have included in Appendix, Table 'A', brief synopses of the tours with regard to factors which influence temperature including distance from the ocean, elevation, and time of year.

We highly recommend the books and maps in the Reading List to supplement your knowledge and enjoyment of mountain biking San Diego.

SAN DIEGO'S COASTAL CANYONS, *including Rose, San Clemente, Los Peñasquitos, and Tecolote, generally host perennial streams and offer many dozens of miles of exploration and loop trip possibilities.* - LL

Useful Telephone Numbers

Area Code 619 unless otherwise noted

AAA (American Automobile Association)	233-1000
Agua Caliente County Park	765-1188
All Emergencies	911
AMTRAK (bikes on selected trains)	(800) USA-RAIL
Anza-Borrego Desert State Park	
Visitor Center	767-4205
Headquarters	767-5311
Bicycling San Diego Magazine (Dan Gindling)	454-1717
Bureau of Land Management (El Centro)	353-1060
California Highway Patrol (non-emergency)	283-6331
Cuyamaca State Park	765-0755
Lake Cuyamaca Recreational District	765-0515
Lake Poway	679-4393
Los Coyotes Indian Reservation	782-3269
Los Peñasquitos Canyon Preserve	533-4067
Map Centre (San Diego)	291-3830
Marian Bear Park	525-8281
Mission Trails Regional Park	533-4051
Northeast Rural Bus (has bike racks)	765-0145
Ocotillo Wells State Vehicular Recreation Area	
(OWSVRA)	767-3545/5391
Palomar Mountain State Park	765-0755
San Diego County Bicycle Coalition	685-7742
San Diego County Parks Department	565-3600
	694-3049
San Diego County Sheriff (non-emergency)	565-5200
San Diego Mountain Bike Club	281-3103
San Diego Museum of Natural History	232-3821
San Diego Pedal Guide (Linda Price)	266-0170
San Diego Regional Transit Center	
(bikes on bus)	233-3004
San Diego Trolley (Metro Transit System)	239-2644
Sierra Club/Bicycle Section	338-8420
Sunbelt Publications	258-4911
Tecolote Canyon	525-8281
Tijuana Estuary State Preserve	575-3613
Torrey Pines State Reserve	755-2063
USFS - Cleveland National Forest HQ.	673-6180
USFS - Descanso District (Alpine)	445-6235
USFS - Palomar District (Ramona)	788-0250
Weather - Surf and Beach	221-8884
Weather/San Diego County Highway Info.	289-1212

POND NEAR DESCANSO JUNCTION represents the serendipity of surprises that awaits the mountain bike explorer in the outback of America's finest county. - LL

Part II

Tours, Trips, and Maps

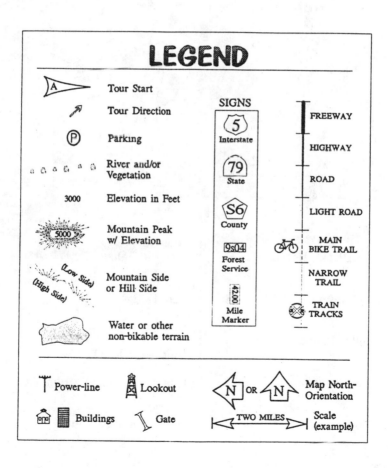

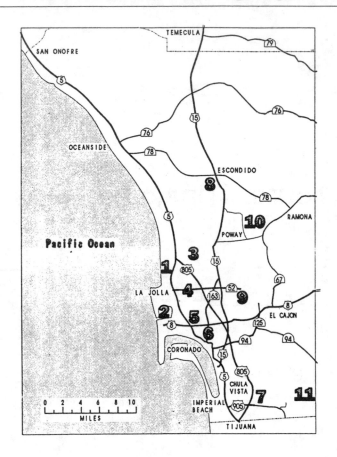

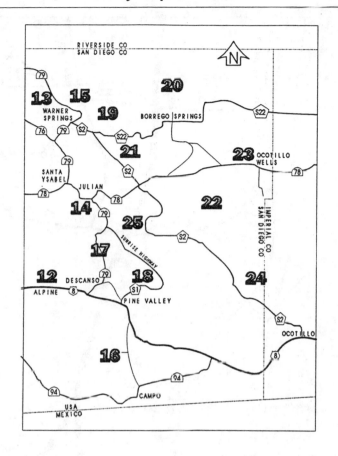

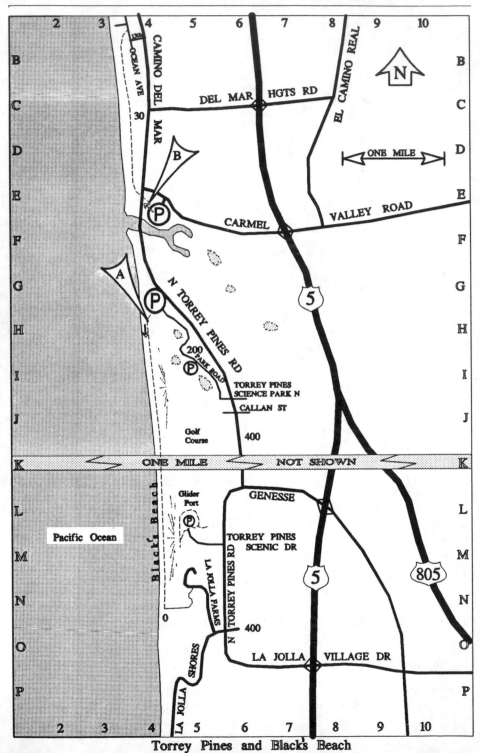

Torrey Pines and Black's Beach

Tour No.:   1

Title: Torrey Pines, Black's Beach to Del Mar

Overview:

This tour follows a stunning strip of coastline that utilizes all of a mountain bike's capabilities. Fat tires should glide over wet sand with unexpected ease, although submarine activity in salt water, and dry sand in the chain and gears must be cleaned out immediately after the trip. The route affords curb hops on curious detours and exciting approaches to the edges of cliffs. With correct usage of the sophisticated design of the mountain bike, this tour can make joyful, but safe little kids of us!

Trip No. 1A: Torrey Pines, Blacks Beach

Length/Time: Nine miles; two hours round trip

Season: Any season. low tide is the priority consideration

Difficulty: Two stars

Trail Surface: Wet sand, 50%; public roads, 40%; steep pavement (no cars), 10%

Trail Grade: Climb: 500 feet; average grade, 2.1%

General:

This trip combines the beauty of the beach from the sand itself, to the views from the tops of 35-story cliffs, towering straight up from the shoreline. You will see hang gliders overhead at Blacks Beach and black sand with gold flecks glittering below (especially dazzling at low tide in sunlight). On the cliffs above Torrey Pines State Park you will find pine trees and some strange geologic formations. The birds'-eye view of the ocean is awesome. The ride on wet sand can be exacting. The challenge is to find those areas of correct dampness that are firmest while at the same time outpacing the breaking waves! To encounter the largest widths of damp sand, try to plan the beach leg of this trip when the tide is going OUT. NOTE: THE BEACH SECTION OF THIS TRIP WILL BE UNDERWATER FROM ABOUT ONE HOUR BEFORE, TO ONE HOUR AFTER HIGH TIDE. CALL BEACH WEATHER AND SURF REPORT FOR DAILY TIDE SCHEDULES: 221-8884. The best riding time is one hour BEFORE LOW TIDE. One other challenge of this trip is the paved lifeguard road from the beach which runs steeply up to the bluffs above (N, 4) to (N, 5).

Logistics:

This trip is located between La Jolla and Del Mar. Exit I-5 at Carmel Valley Road. Turn left (south) on North Torrey Pines Road (S-21) and cross Peñasquitos Lagoon. Turn right into the beach parking lot (fee). Parking may be available on North Torrey Pines Road between (F, 4) and (G, 4). Parking may also be available at Torrey Pines State Reserve ($4.00 fee) (G, 4) and (I, 5), and also at the Glider Port (L, 5).

Miles from Start	Route Directions: 1A - Torrey Pines, Black's Beach	Miles to End
0.0	From the south end of the parking lot on the beach at [G,4] a dirt road leads to the beach. Head south on damp sand.	9.0
1.0	Flat Rock. Carry bikes carefully over the rock shelf here. (Observe Eocene fossil shellfish embedded in the sandstone).	8.0
2.7	This general vicinity is the most popular section of Black's Beach. You should see hang gliders overhead. [L,4]	6.3
3.9	Take the steep paved lifeguard access road from the beach to La Jolla Farms Road above. [N,4]	5.1
4.3	Turn right on La Jolla Farms Road.	4.7
4.9	Turn left on La Jolla Shores Drive.	4.1
5.0	Turn left on North Torrey Pines Road (S-21).	4.0
5.8	Pass Torrey Pines Scenic Drive on the left. This is the road to the glider port. (Option: Turn left here and check out the glider port. There are some great aerial views of the ocean. This detour is not added to trip mileage.)	3.2
6.2	Turn left to stay on North Torrey Pines Road. [K,6]	2.8
7.7	Pass Torrey Pines Science Park North on the left. This leads to an old winding road that goes through the Torrey Pines State Reserve. (Option: Turn left (west) here, then take Torrey Pines Park Road north. This detour is not added to trip mileage.)	1.3
9.0	Back to start. (At this point you can continue north on North Torrey Pines Road and add on Trip 1B)	0.0

Trip No.1B: Del Mar Beach

Length/Time: Four miles; 1/2 hour round-trip.

Season: Summer recommended

Difficulty: Two stars

Trail Surface: Hard dirt, 50%; public roads, 40%; stones, 10%

Trail Grade: Climb: 200 feet; average grade, 1.9%

General:

It is suggested this tour be taken as a supplement to Trip A. It is a short spin up the beach along the railroad tracks, usually accompanied by a few joggers. The route then passes through the town of Del Mar.

Logistics

Exit I-5 at Carmel Valley Road and head west. Parking may be available on Carmel Valley Road between [E,4] and [E,5], or at the Torrey Pines State Reserve parking lot at [E,4] ($4 fee).

Miles from Start	Route Directions: 1B - Del Mar Beach	Miles to End
0.00	Take the bike path from the northwest corner of the parking lot. [E,4]	3.96
0.09	Pass under bridge then stay to the right.	3.87
0.14	Go through gate on the right and head uphill. The trail heads north along the railroad tracks.	3.82
1.72	Trail ends; turn right heading south on Ocean Boulevard. [B,3.5]	2.24
1.94	Turn left heading uphill on 13th Street.	2.02
2.06	Turn right heading south on Camino Del Mar. [B,4]	1.90
3.31	Turn left heading east on Carmel Valley Road. [E,4]	0.65
3.71	Turn right back into parking lot.	0.25
3.96	Back to start.	0.00

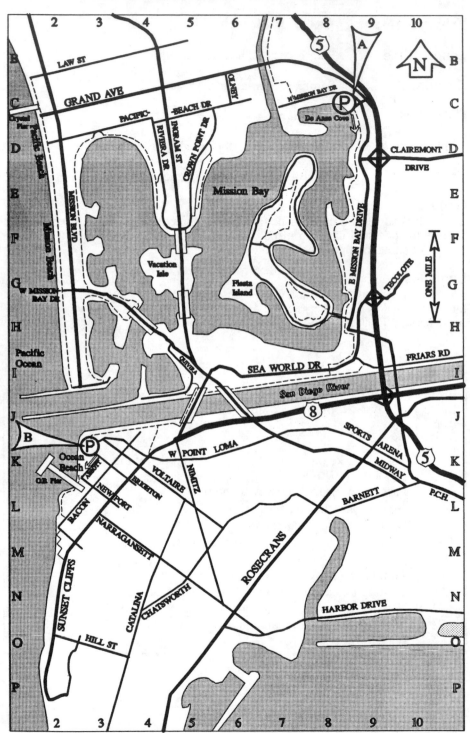

Mission Bay and Sunset Cliffs

Tour No.:   2

Title: Mission Bay, Sunset Cliffs

Overview:
Mission Bay is one of the most unique areas in our beautiful city. Year-round activities abound. The bays and ocean are popular with wind surfers and sailing enthusiasts. Volleyball, rollerskating, and surfing are popular along the beach. Jet skiing, over-the-line baseball, and kite flying activities are seen at Fiesta Island. Ocean Beach and areas to the south afford ample opportunities for fishermen and tide-pool explorers. In addition, bike trails in and around this area make it possible to stay off the busy thoroughfares and out of traffic to a large degree. This means cleaner air and better viewing!

Trip No. 2A: Mission Bay Loop (clockwise)

Length/Time: 12 miles; two hours round-trip

Season: Any season. (In summer, week days recommended.)

Difficulty: One star (easy)

Trail Surface: Paved bike trails, 65%; public roads, 30%; mild off-road trails (optional), 5%

Trail Grade: Climb: 100 feet; average grade, unnoticeable

General:
This is the most pavement-oriented of all the tours in this book. The area abounds in concrete bike paths making this a good beginner's trip. There are a few off-road trails on Fiesta Island, but this area is geared more towards light pedaling and people-watching - especially along the boardwalk.

Logistics:
The tour area is at the west end of I-8. Exit I-5 at Clairemont Drive. Proceed west along Clairemont Drive one block to its end, then turn right onto East Mission Bay Drive. Parking is available at De Anza Cove (C, 8). If you start the tour on the east side of the bay, the prevailing west winds will become tail winds on the last stretch of the tour.

Miles from Start	Route Directions: 2A Mission Bay Loop (clockwise)	Miles to End
0.00	Head south from De Anza Cove on the sidewalk on the east side of Mission Bay. [C,8]	2.07
2.61	Cross entrance to Fiesta Island. [H,8] Stay on sidewalk. (Option: From this point you can turn right and explore Fiesta Island. There are a few off-road trails as indicated on the map. This detour is not added to trip mileage.)	9.46
2.74	Turn right on Sea World Drive. (Stay on sidewalk.)	9.33
3.00	Pass Friars Road on the left.	9.07
3.30	Cross over Sea World Drive through opening in the median strip and continue west (right) along the San Diego River levee on bike path on the south side of Sea World Drive.[I,8]	8.77
4.06	Stay left on bike path and go under two bridges. [I,6]	8.01
4.55	Bike path ends, turn right on Quivera Way east and then north. [I,5]	7.52
4.65	Pass bike path to Ocean Beach on the right. (Option: At this point you can easily add on trip 2B (Sunset Cliffs) by turning right (southwest) on this path and crossing the Sunset Cliffs Boulevard bridge heading southwest. Then take the path west that runs along the south side of the San Diego River. It ends at Ocean Beach where you can follow directions for Trip 2B. This detour is not added to trip mileage.)	7.42
5.22	Turn left heading northwest on West Mission Bay Drive from Quivira Way. [H,5]	6.85
6.05	Just past the Bahia Hotel turn right heading north on the Bay Side Boardwalk, (A couple blocks before (east of) Mission Boulevard). [G,3] (Option: If you want an ocean view continue west and take the Ocean Side Boardwalk north. Cross back over to the Bay Side Boardwalk a few blocks south of Pacific Beach Drive. This detour not added to trip mileage.). Boardwalk curves east.	6.02
7.46	Just past the Catamaran Hotel you must take a 2 block detour because of a short break in the Bayside Boardwalk. [D,3] Take Briarfield Drive north and stay to the right. It leads back south to the boardwalk.	4.61
7.62	Back to the boardwalk which now curves south.	4.45
8.36	Heading south now, watch for a sharp left turn on a paved path that heads steeply uphill to the road above. Then turn right heading south and then east on Riviera Drive. [E,4]	3.71

Miles from Start	Route Directions: 2A Mission Bay Loop (clockwise)	Miles to End
8.90	Cross Ingraham Street heading east, then curve north. (Riviera Drive turns into Crown Point Drive here). [F,5]	3.17
9.12	Turn right on Corona Oriente, towards the water.	2.95
9.26	Turn right into parking lot, get to the sidewalk and turn left.	2.81
9.30	Turn left on sidewalk.	2.77
9.75	Turn right out of parking lot onto Corona Oriente. [D,5]	2.32
9.90	Turn right on Crown Point Drive. (Following bike path signs for a while.)	2.17
10.27	Turn right on Pacific Beach Drive. [C,5]	1.80
10.42	Turn left heading north on Olney Street. [C,6]	1.65
10.68	Turn right on Grand Avenue.	1.39
11.03	Get up on the sidewalk when you get to the high school, heading east along Grand Avenue still.	1.04
11.13	Just after crossing a small river, turn right on a paved bike path along the river heading south. [B,7]	0.94
11.44	Bike path ends on North Mission Bay Drive, turn left heading east.	0.63
12.07	Back to start	0.00

MISSION BAY is laced with many miles of paved bicycle and walking paths. - LL

Trip No.: 2B   Sunset Cliffs

Length/Time: Six miles; one hour round trip

Season: Summer: weekends recommended

Difficulty: Two stars

Trail Surface: Public road, 90%; off-road (optional), 10%

Trail Grade: Climb: 300 feet; average grade, 2.0%

General:

This is a very easy ride designed as a supplement to Trip 2A, but by itself it includes the attractions of Ocean Beach Pier and Sunset Cliffs. Optional activities here include trying to ride the rocks just south of the pier.

Logistics:

This area is located at the west end of I-8 freeway. Take I-8 to its end and bear left in the right lane to Sunset Cliffs Boulevard. Turn right onto West Point Loma Blvd. and follow its curve around to the Ocean Beach parking lot [K, 3].

Miles from Start	Route Directions: 2B - Sunset Cliffs, Ocean Beach	Miles to End
0.00	Head east on Brighton Avenue from the south end of the Ocean Beach parking lot. [K,3]	5.58
0.12	Turn right on Abbott Street.	5.46
0.39	Take the sidewalk under the Ocean Beach Pier before Abbott turns left into Newport Avenue. [K,3]	5.19
0.47	Pass under the pier and continue on sidewalk winding around to the ocean.	5.11
0.57	Descend steps to the rock ledges. (If the rocks are too challenging, you can go back and take streets heading south and continue with the trip later at "mile 1.51.")	5.01
0.80	Carry your bike up the steps to the street. Once on the street, head south (right) and stay on streets as close to the ocean as possible until you end up at Sunset Cliffs Blvd.	4.78
1.51	Turn right heading south on Sunset Cliffs Boulevard. There will be plenty of places to pull off and get a great view. Occasionally there is a stretch of dirt trail on the right side of the road, but most of them are hardly worth lifting your bike over the guardrail for.	4.07

Miles from Start	Route Directions: 2B - Sunset Cliffs, Ocean Beach	Miles to End
2.79	Sunset Cliffs makes a left turn away from the ocean and turns into Ladera Street. This is the designated turn-around point for this trip. (Trails in Sunset Cliffs Park to the south of here have been closed to bikes.)	2.79
5.58	Back to start.	0.00

SUNSET CLIFFS features rocky shelves, traversable at lower tides, cut into ancient marine terraces. - LL

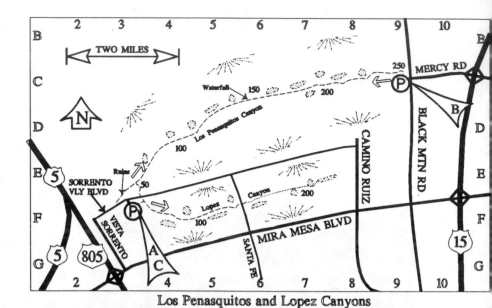

Los Penasquitos and Lopez Canyons

LOS PEÑASQUITOS CANYON is incised into the Kearny Mesa marine terrace, providing the drainage between Poway and Sorrento Valley. - SB

Tour No.: 3

Title: Los Peñasquitos Canyon Preserve

Overview:

This area has received much attention with regard to the controversial issue of mountain bike access. Although signs at the entry points notify visitors that mountain biking is allowed only on the main wide dirt trail on the south side of the stream, a few riders continue to blaze the single track trails and cross the stream to get to the northern trails. These few rebels may ruin it for the rest of us. We are limited to the wide trail because it gets crowded here with hikers and horseback riders. Passing them on a bike is a hassle anywhere but on the wide trail. Please remember that here, as well as everywhere else, mountain bikers have the least "right-of-way." We must yield to every other type of trail user.

On the lighter side, this is a beautiful area with plenty of large trees and wildlife. A friend of mine was nearly stampeded here, right in front of me, by a family of deer! A stream runs through the main valley of the preserve and falls over a colorful rock formation at the half-way point of the main trail. Trip 3A and 3B divide Los Peñasquitos Canyon into halves which can be added together as a single tour. Trip 3C, Lopez Canyon to the south, also very colorful, is rocky and much less traveled than Los Peñasquitos Canyon. This sonorous name reportedly derives from the Spanish "small, round rocks" or "place of little cliffs," (Stein).

Trip No. 3A: West Half, Los Peñasquitos Canyon Preserve

Length/Time: Six miles to waterfalls and return; one hour round trip

Season: All year

Difficulty: Two stars

Trail Surface: Wide, graded dirt road, 100%

Trail Grade: Climb: 400 feet; average grade, 2.5%

General:

From its west end, the ride through this grand valley provides a panorama of cliffs and unfolding tributary canyons. At dawn cattle stare in the cold mist. Then sunlight slices over the canyon rim, cutting into the cool, damp shadows and creating dry, warm air pockets which alternately chill and thaw as you pass.

Logistics:

The canyon is located between Sorrento Valley and Mira Mesa. Exit I-805 at Mira Mesa Blvd. and proceed east (P,11). From Mira Mesa Blvd.turn left onto the frontage road, Vista Sorrento Parkway, and proceed north. After one mile, turn right at the stop sign onto Sorrento Valley Boulevard. One mile from Vista Sorrento Parkway, on the right (south) side of Sorrento Valley Boulevard, is a parking lot for the preserve.

Miles from Start	Route Directions: 3A - Los Peñasquitos West Half	Miles to End
0.00	Take the trail on the east side of the parking lot. [F,4]	5.52
0.06	Turn left at the fork heading north. You will go under a bridge, then up over a hill.	5.46
0.48	Turn right heading east on the main trail. [E,4]	5.04
2.76	Arrive at waterfall on the left (north) side of the trail. [C,6]	
	Check it out and return the same way you came. (Option: From here you could continue 2.8 miles to the east end of the main canyon and then head back (Trip 3B). (This 5.6 mile detour not added to trip mileage).	2.76
5.52	Back to start, try Trip 3C below.	0.00

Trip No. 3B: East Half, Los Peñasquitos Canyon Preserve

Length/Time: Six miles to waterfalls and return; one hour two-way trip

Season: All year

Difficulty: One star

Trail Surface: Wide, graded dirt road, 100%

Trail Grade: Climb: 200 feet; average grade, 1.3%

General:

The end of the Preserve is usually the most crowded. One reason is that the horse camp and staging area are located here. From here to the waterfalls midway, the canyon differs from the sparse but picturesque trees of the west end. The shrubbery is denser and wildlife is more plentiful. Deer may be seen in this section of the canyon, as well as hawks, kites, and other birds. The trail is one of the easiest bike trails.

Logistics:

The east end of the Preserve is located in Mira Mesa. Exit I-15 at Mercy

Road and proceed west. The west end of Mercy Road goes directly into parking lot for east end of the preserve, after intersecting Black Mountain Road.

Miles from Start	Route Directions: 3B - Los Penasquitos East Half	Miles to End
0.00	Take the main trail west from north side of parking lot. [C,9]	6.20
0.50	Pass riparian restoration area on the right.	5.70
3.10	Arrive at waterfall on right (north) side of trail [C,6] return same way you came. (Option: Here you could continue 2.8 miles to west end main canyon then head back (Trip 3A). (This 5.6 mile detour not added to trip mileage).	3.10
6.20	Back to start.	0.00

Trip No. 3C: Los Peñasquitos: Lopez Canyon

Length/Time: Four miles; 45 minutes two-way trip

Season: All year

Difficulty: Two stars

Trail Surface: Wide dirt trail 50%, rocky wash 50%

Trail Grade: Climb: 200 feet; average grade, 1.9%

General:

This trip is best taken as a supplement to Trip 3A when you get back from the waterfalls and still have energy left. It is a short ride through scenery similar to Los Peñasquitos Canyon, although much less crowded. The trail becomes rockier the farther east you ride. By the time you cross underneath the Camino Santa Fe bridge you may have had enough rocks, but you can proceed quite a bit further. Some maps show this as Cuervo Canyon (Sp. "crow").

Logistics:

Same as for Trip 3A above.

Miles from Start	Route Directions: 3C - Lopez Canyon	Miles to End
0.00	Take the trail on the east side of the parking lot. [F,4]	3.80
0.06	Turn right at the fork.	3.74
0.54	Pass Old Lopez Road on the right, which climbs to Pacific Center Blvd.	3.26

Miles from Start	Route Directions: 3C Lopez Canyon	Miles to End
1.43	Start of the river rock. (Trail gets progressively rockier)	2.37
1.90	Camino Santa Fe bridge. This is designated turn-around for trip. [F,6] (You can go further up Lopez to Montongo St.).	1.90
3.80	Back to start at Sorrento Valley Blvd.	0.00

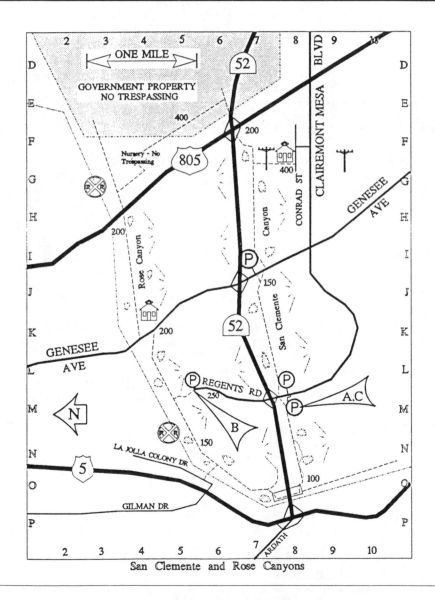

San Clemente and Rose Canyons

Tour No.:   4

Title: San Clemente and Rose Canyons

Overview:

Beautiful oaks, willows and gnarled sycamore trees are the main attractions in mid San Clemente Canyon - also known as Marian Bear Memorial Park. The stream which feeds this greenery adds to the scenic beauty. It can also be one of the area's challenges! The Rose Canyon traverse is the least difficult of the two. It is quieter, and features the main line of the Santa Fe Railroad instead of the Route 52 freeway of San Clemente Canyon. Near I-805 in both canyons, the trail is the streambed. This results in a very rocky ride, but what could be a better place to work on balancing skills, or to break in new equipment such as that new gel seat, or helmet? Because of the diversity of trails and challenges, this tour has been divided into three trips.

Trip No. 4A: San Clemente Canyon

Length/Time: Seven miles; 1 hour two-way trip

Season: All year

Difficulty: Two stars

Trail Surface: Wide, smooth dirt, 80%; river stones, 15%; steep single-track, 5% (optional)

Trail Grade: Climb: 200 feet; average grade, 1.1%

General:

Do you have any "intermediate level" mountain cyclist friends visiting? This is a fun place to take them. It might be considered the site of the finest rides in town. In summer the stream is dry and features little but stones. However, after a winter rain it can become a raging torrent. The trail and stream meet several times and it can be fun crisscrossing - depending on the water level, of course.

Logistics:

This area lies parallel to the Route 52 freeway and is on the freeway's south side in Clairemont. Exit at Clairemont Mesa Boulevard to the south. Parking is available at the lot just west of Clairemont Mesa Boulevard [M, 8].

Miles from Start	Route Directions: 4A - San Clemente Canyon	Miles to End
0.00	From the parking lot, head east through the tunnel underneath Clairemont Mesa Boulevard. [M,8] Continue east through the next parking lot to the trail on the east end.	6.74
1.15	Stay to the right and take the stream bed under the Genesee Avenue bridge. [I,7]	5.59
2.16	Pass access trail to Conrad Street on the right.	4.58
2.43	Arrive at Interstate 805 bridge. This is the official turn-around point for this trip. [E,7] Do not go east under I-805, to avoid trespassing onto NAS Miramar.	4.31
4.86	Back to start. [M,8] Continue west on the trail to explore the west end of San Clemente Canyon.	1.88
5.80	Reach the stream on the west end of San Clemente Canyon then head back the same way that you came. [O,8] (Option: Cross the stream and there is a trail that runs south, parallel to the train tracks, for about a mile. Take that to its end and back. This detour is not added to trip mileage).	0.94
6.74	Back to start.	0.00

ROSE CANYON trail, like so many paralleling San Diego stream courses, is arched by noble Sycamores. - LL

Trip No. 4B: Rose Canyon

Length/Time: Eight miles; 1 hour two-way trip

Season: All year

Difficulty: Two stars

Trail Surface: Wide, smooth dirt, 85%; rocky, 10%; single-track, 5%

Trail Grade: Climb: 300 feet; average grade, 1.4%

General:

Rose Canyon is very similar to San Clemente Canyon, but provides a simpler ride due to fewer stream crossings and generally wider trails. There are more joggers along this route. The railroad runs along the north border of the canyon. You may see a train or two.

Logistics:

This area lies north of the Route 52 freeway and the San Clemente Canyon area. Exit the Route 52 freeway at Regents Road and proceed north on Regents Road. Parking is available at the north end of Regents Road [M, 5].

Miles from Start	Route Directions: 4B - Rose Canyon	Miles to End
0.00	From the north end of Regents Road, take the trail downhill that runs next to a cement ditch. [M,6]	7.98
0.21	Turn right in Rose Canyon. [M,5]	7.77
0.97	Turn left on Genesee Avenue; proceed tostop light. [K,4]	7.01
1.05	Cross Genesee at the light and the trail continues on the left (north) side of the entrance to University High School.	6.93
2.35	Arrive at the Interstate 805 bridge. This is the official turn-around point for this trip. [H,4] It is advised that you not go east under I-805, to avoid trespassing.	5.63
4.49	Pass access trail to Regents Road that you came down, on the left, [M,5] and proceed to the west end of Rose Canyon.	3.49
5.31	Pass access trail to La Jolla Colony Drive on right. [N,6]	2.67
6.13	Arrive at north end of a cement ditch that runs underneath Highway 52. [O,7] Head back the same way you came. (Option: Near the south end ofcement ditch is a trail that runs south, parallel to the train tracks, for about a mile.Take that to end and back.This detour not added to trip mileage.)	1.85
7.98	Back to start.	0.00

Trip No. 4C: Both Canyons

Length/Time: Six miles; one hour round trip

Season: All year

Difficulty: Three stars

Trail Surface: Wide dirt trails, 75%; public road, 15%; rocks, 5%;
                     single track trail, 5%.

Trail Grade: Climb: 500 feet; average grade, 3.2%

General:

One of the best tours in town! It takes in the beauty of both canyons with the option of adding on more trip distance by exploring each of the canyons' eastern ends between Genesee Avenue and Interstate 805.

Logistics:

Exit the Route 52 freeway south onto Clairemont Mesa Boulevard. Parking is available at the lot on the west side (M, 8).

Miles from Start	Route Directions: 4C - San Clemente, Rose Canyon Round Trip	Miles to End
0.00	Head west on the trail from the edge of parking lot. [M,8]	5.83
0.94	Reach the stream on the west end of San Clemente. A steep section of single track trail, running north near the freeway fence, is probably the easiest way to get to the cement ditch that you must take north from here. [O,8]	4.89
1.10	Reach north end of cement ditch, when you get on dirt trail again, take a left heading north onwide dirt road. [O,7]	4.73
1.25	The uphill starts, the only through-trail on this side of the railroad tracks is narrow and slanted.	4.58
1.92	Pass access trail on left to La Jolla Colony Drive. [N,6]	3.91
2.74	Pass access trail on right that leads to Regents Road. [M,5]	3.09
3.50	Turn right heading southeast and uphill on Genesee Avenue and descend into San Clemente Canyon. [K,5]	2.33
4.68	After you cross under Highway 52, you will see a parking lot on the other (east) side of the road. At this point drop off to the right side of the road, onto the trail heading west, in San Clemente Canyon. [I,8]	1.15
5.74	Pass under Clairemont Mesa Boulevard. [M,8]	0.09
5.83	Back to start.	0.00

SAN CLEMENTE CANYON is threaded by a sparkling creek much of the year. - LL

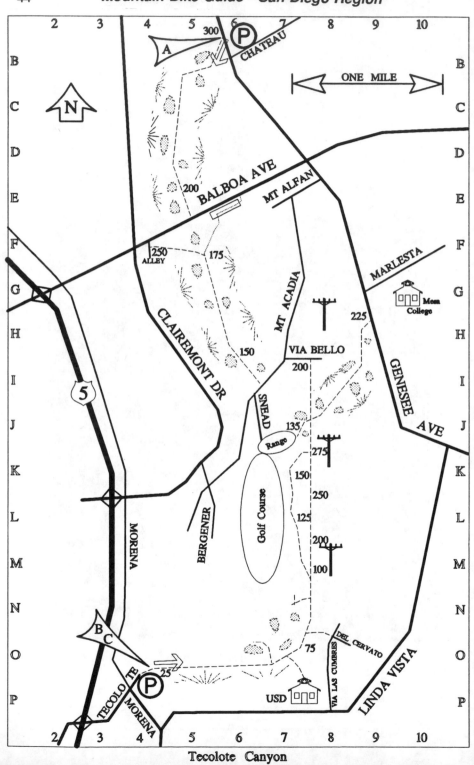

Tecolote Canyon

Tour No.:   5

Title: Tecolote Canyon

Overview
This nature preserve contrasts sharply with the dense residential   area surrounding it. Once in the canyon, the walls shut out all of the commotion from the mesa above. There is an abundance of beautiful vegetation here, supported by two streams that usually have water year-round. There are several nooks that are completely surrounded by shade and the sound of babbling water. Tecolote Canyon is especially appealing because of its central location. Its size and road layout can provide a variety of trip possibilites. Tours 5A and 5B traverse the northern and southern halves of the main canyon. Trip 5C adds together Trips 5A, 5B and a stretch of road, to make a round trip of the area.

Trip No. 5A: Northern Half, Tecolote Canyon

Length/Time: Six miles; one-hour two-way trip

Season: All year

Difficulty: Two stars

Trail Surface: Single-track trail, 90%; street, 10%

Trail Grade: Climb: 200 feet; average grade, 1.3%

General:
The trail through the northern half of the canyon follows the original pioneering path through the area. It is narrow and experiences less traffic than in other canyon areas. The trail becomes bumpy in some sections. The trail is split into two sections by Balboa Avenue. Balboa has a divider running down its center, and a detour up to Clairemont Drive must be taken to go around it. Finding the trailhead to the second section at [F,4] can be a little difficult because it is in an alley and hidden behind a guardrail and some bushes.

Logistics:
The canyon is located in Clairemont. Exit freeways I-5 or I-805 at Balboa Avenue. Proceed to Genesee Avenue and head north. Parking is available on Chateau Drive (B, 6).

Miles from Start	Route Directions: 5A - Tecolote Canyon Northern Half	Miles to End
0.00	Head south and downhill on the trail off the west side of Genesee, just north of Chateau Drive. [B,6]	6.00
1.34	Turn right,uphill, heading west, on Balboa Avenue.[F,5]	4.66
1.70	At Clairemont Drive, cross Balboa Avenue and head back east on Balboa for one block. (A divider down the middle of Balboa prevents you from cutting across earlier.)	4.30
1.79	Turn right into the alley on the east side of the shops. About 20 feet up on the left will be the trail on the back-side of a guardrail. [F,4] It is a single track trail and heads downhill into the canyon.	4.21
1.96	Cross the stream and take the trail to the right heading south.	4.04
2.33	Pass an access trail on the left.	3.67
3.00	Arrive at Mt. Acadia. This is designated turn-around point for this trip. [I,6] (Option: for variety, turn left and uphill on Mt. Acadia, right on Mt. Alfan, and left on Genesee, back to start. This detour not added to trip mileage).	3.00
6.00	Back to start.	0.00

TECOLOTE CANYON, unlike most of San Diego's east-west stream-formed canyons, trends north and south as a fault controlled feature and is related to the major Rose Canyon fault system. - LL

Trip No. 5B: Southern Half, Tecolote Canyon

Length/Time: Five miles; one-hour two-way trip

Season: All year

Difficulty: Four stars

Trail Surface: Wide, flat dirt, 50%; super steep, but wide dirt, 40%; single-track (optional), 10%

Trail Grade: Climb: 700 feet; average grade, 5.3%

General:
The trail starts as a mild path along the canal at the south end of the canyon. Conversely, as the trail proceeds north and becomes the powerline road, it becomes extremely challenging! Excellent overhead greenery is seen on the trail from (H, 8) to (J, 7). Many stream crossings can present difficulties.

Logistics:
This portion of the canyon is located east of Mission Bay. Exit I-5 at Tecolote Road. Follow Tecolote Road east to its end. Parking is available at the Parks and Recreation Department parking lot, (P, 4).

Miles from Start	Route Directions: 5B - Tecolote Canyon Southern Half	Miles to End
0.00	Head east on the wide dirt trail from the east end of Tecolote Road, past the baseball diamonds. [O,4]	4.96
0.06	Pass through gate.	4.90
0.97	Pass trail on the right to University of San Diego. [O,7]	3.99
1.45	Stay right (east) along golf course for easiest trail. The serious hills start here. [M,8]	3.51
2.14	Forced to go uphill on wide trail heading east, (no other trail will take you further north). [K,7]	2.82
2.33	Turn left heading north on power-line road down a severe drop-off, (then a severe climb, and another drop-off!).	2.63
2.48	Come to an intersection with single track trail at bottom of a lush canyon. [J,8] This is the designated turn-around point for this trip. (Option: here you can turn left (west), to west end of single track trail, and see a shady pool. Or turn right (east) and explore to the east until trail ends at Genesee. See Trip 5C directions to take Genesee/Linda Vista back to start, if desired.These detours not added into trip mileage).	2.48
4.96	Back to start.	0.00

Trip No. 5C: Tecolote Canyon, Round Trip

Length/Time: 13 miles; two hours round trip

Season: All year

Difficulty: Four stars

Trail Surface: Public roads, 50%; single track trail, 30%; wide dirt trail, 10%; steep dirt trail, 10%

Trail Grade: Climb: 1000 feet; average grade, 3%

General:

Basically, this is Trip 5B one-way, added to Trip 5A one-way, then a stretch of road is added to get you back to start.

Logistics:

This portion of the canyon is located east of Mission Bay. Exit I-5 at Tecolote Road. Follow Tecolote Road east to its end. Parking is available at the Parks and Recreation Department parking lot, (P, 4).

TECOLOTE CANYON (Sp. "owl") features hidden grottoes of fern, ivy, and creatures of the coastal riparian community. - SB

Miles from Start	Route Description: 5C - Tecolote Canyon Round Trip	Miles to End
0.00	Head east on the wide dirt trail from the east end of Tecolote Road, past the baseball diamonds. [O,4]	12.70
0.06	Pass through gate.	12.64
0.97	Pass trail on the right to University of San Diego. [O,7]	11.73
1.45	Stay right (east) along golf course for easiest trail. The serious hills start here. [M,8]	11.25
2.14	Forced to go uphill on wide trail heading east, (no other trail will take you further north). [K,7]	10.56
2.33	Turn left heading north on the power-line road down severe drop-off, (then a severe climb, and another drop-off!).	10.37
2.48	Come to an intersection with a single track trail at bottom of a lush canyon. [J,8]	10.22
2.50	Cross stream and continue north up steep power-line road.	10.20
2.67	Trail levels out.	10.03
2.79	Turn left (west) on Via Bello. [H,7]	9.91
2.84	Turn left and downhill on Mt. Acadia Boulevard.	9.86
3.17	Turn right on trail heading north. [I,7]	9.53
3.84	Pass access trail on the right.	8.86
4.19	Take left fork of trail down to stream. [F,5]	8.51
4.21	Cross stream and head uphill.	8.49
4.38	Arrive at guardrail at end of trail. Turn right in alley down 20 feet to Balboa, then turn left up to the stop light at Clairemont Drive. [F,4]	8.32
4.47	Cross Clairemont Drive and turn right heading east and downhill on the sidewalk on north side of Balboa Avenue.	8.23
4.83	Turn left heading north on trail off of Balboa Avenue. [F,5]	7.87
6.17	End of trail, turn right (south), on Genesee Avenue.[B,6]	6.53
9.33	Turn right (west) on Linda Vista Road. [K,10]	3.37
11.06	Turn right (north) on Via las Cumbres. [P,8]	1.64
11.52	When you see Del Cervato on the right, the trail will be on the left side of the road. [O,8] Take trail heading down into Tecolote Canyon.	1.18
11.67	Turn left heading south on main trail, (same one you came in on). [O,7]	1.03
12.70	Back to start at Tecolote Park Recreation Center.	0.00

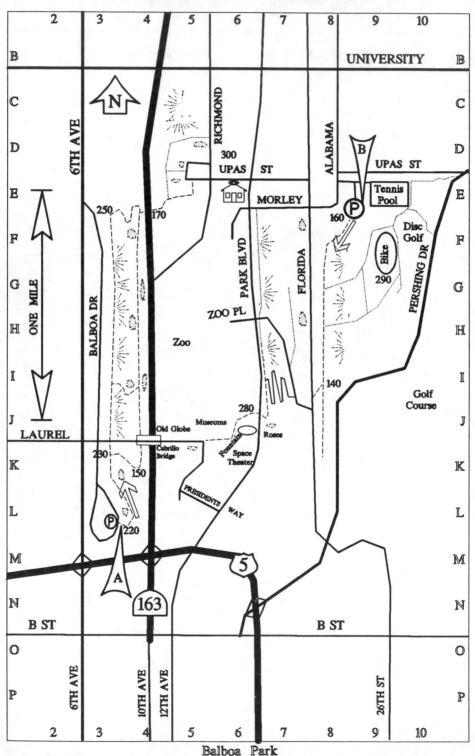

Balboa Park

Tour No.: 6

Title: Balboa Park

Overview:

This 1400 acre park is a popular place, especially on the weekends. Balboa is home to many museums, theaters and of course, the San Diego Zoo. Many years of cultivation have produced a wide range of scenery. From the pine trees along the Route 163 freeway to the native chaparral in Florida Canyon, you will find a huge variety of trees and foliage. There is even a small section of desert landscape which includes saguaro cacti! Sidewalks will take you within sight of other things that the park is known for - its architecture, its beautiful fountain, and, of course, its street performers - musicians, jugglers, and so on. All of these are found at the east end of El Prado which is the easterly extension of Laurel St. in Balboa Park (J, 6). The dirt trails on the west side of the park suffer from overuse. Extreme caution is advised if they are to be used.

Trip No. 6A: West Side, Balboa Park

Length/Time: Four miles; 1/2 hour round trip

Season: All year, weekdays

Difficulty: Two stars

Trail Surface: Sidewalk, 75%; dirt trail, 25%

Trail Grade: Climb: 100 feet; average grade, 0.9%

General:

The west side is the more developed side of the park. Most of the activity takes place on weekends. People watching is part of the park's allure. The most mountain-bikable area is the loop of sidewalks parallel to 6th Avenue and Balboa Drive.

Logistics:

The park is located northeast of downtown. Exit I-5 North at 6th Ave., or exit Route 163 North at Quince. Follow Balboa Drive all the way to the south end of the park where it becomes a one-way street. As it loops around, park just north of the abandoned fire station.

Miles from Start	Route Directions: 6A - Balboa Park West Side	Miles to End
0.00	Take the dirt trail that heads east, then immediately north, around a small grove of pine trees. [L,4]	4.06
0.10	Trail joins with sidewalk, head north.	3.96
0.57	Cross El Prado, continue north on sidewalk. [J/K,3.5]	3.49
1.24	Reach the north boundary of the park, turn right following the sidewalk east, then curving around. [E,3]	2.82
1.30	Sidewalk starts steep winding descent.	2.76
1.40	Pass bridge that goes over Highway 163 on the left. Take the dirt trail heading south along 163. (Option: Take bridge over 163. Turn left (north) as soon as you get across the highway and explore the maze of trails. This detour is not added to trip mileage).	2.66
1.86	Cross extinct freeway ramp. [H,4]	2.20
1.97	Pass trail on the right. [I,4]	2.09
2.00	Cross under Cabrillo Bridge and start uphill.	2.06
2.12	Pass trail on the left.	1.94
2.17	Reach grass nearing top of the hill, walk bike west until you can cut to the right and get on El Prado. [K,3]	1.89
2.25	Head east on El Prado crossing over Cabrillo Bridge.	1.81
2.87	Reach the fountain, near Park Drive. [J,6] This is official turn-around point for trip. Head back west on El Prado.	1.19
3.49	Turn left (south) on Balboa Drive or parallel sidewalk.[J/K,3]	0.57
4.06	Back to start.	0.00

CABRILLO BRIDGE arcs high over Balboa Park's westside bike and foot trail in the canyon which, thanks to thick foliage, seems remote and insulated from busy city traffic just a few yards away. - SB

Trip No. 6B: East Side, Balboa Park

Length/Time: Two miles, 1/2 hour round trip

Season: All year

Difficulty: Three stars

Trail Surface: Single-track, 70%; sidewalk, 10%; public roads, 20%

Trail Grade: Climb: 300 feet; average grade, 5.7%

General:

This is the more primitive side of the park with Florida Canyon being very undeveloped. It's not quite as crowded here, but the trails are much more difficult due to rocks and overgrown vegetation. The canyon wall on the west side of Florida Drive was once too thick with vegetation for biking. However, a recent fire has exposed the old trails and new ones are evolving from use.

Logistics:

The area is located in North Park. Exit I-5 at Pershing Drive. Proceed on Pershing north to Florida Drive and turn left. Go north to Morley Field Drive and turn right. Once up the hill, turn right into the parking lot. Immediately turn right and descend to the lower parking lot south of the tennis courts (E, 9).

Miles from Start	Route Description: 6B - Balboa Park East Side	Miles to End
0.00	From the small parking lot on the west side of the tennis courts, head across the grass to the southwest corner.[F,8]	2.00
0.07	Trail starts by a wooden work-out station. Take the most gradual one downhill towards Florida Street. The easiest trail runs parallel to Florida Street.	1.93
0.60	Turn off trail onto Florida Street when you see Zoo Place coming down to Florida Street on right.[I,8] Head up Zoo Place and as soon as possible get on sidewalk, (left side).	1.40
0.73	Turn left and uphill on a steep switch-back sidewalk.	1.27
0.92	Arrive at top of sidewalk. Walk bike west through desert garden to sidewalk along Park Drive. (They issue citations for riding bike through garden) [I,7] (Option: Once on sidewalk turn left (south) and walk bike across bridge to explore center of park .This detour is not added to trip mileage).	1.08
0.96	Head north on the sidewalk along Park Drive, you will soon be forced onto the pavement.	1.04

Miles from Start	Route Description: 6B - Balboa Park East Side	Miles to End
1.12	Cross Zoo Place, at this point you can jump up onto the grass and take a faded trail right along the canyon edge. Wood chips recently placed here take some of the fun out of this.	0.88
1.52	Turn right and downhill on Morley Field Drive. [E,6]	0.48
2.00	Back to start.	0.00

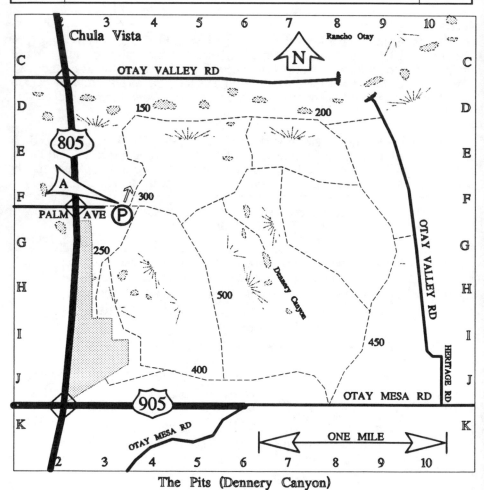

The Pits (Dennery Canyon)

Tour No.:   7

Title: Otay Mesa (Dennery Canyon, or "The Pits")

Overview:
This is one of the last areas to remain open to motorized off-roading in the city. It is known to most who go there as simply - "The Pits." It was so named because of the many steep canyon walls that appear as pits when viewed from the top edges of the canyon. Actually, the area is part of Dennery Canyon. It is a rather small area, but very interesting for several reasons besides its close-to-the-city location. Motorcycles and 4 x 4's have made innumerable trails which run in every direction (many more than could be shown on the map). As might be expected, some of these provide the biker with real challenges. Therefore, you will almost always be able to travel in any direction you wish, knowing at the same time that there are different routes, maybe easier or maybe more difficult, by which to get there. The Otay River (generally a stream) runs along the northern border with riparian vegetation. Consider weekday visits to avoid dust and noise pollution from OHV's.

Trip No. 7A:	Perimeter Zigzag
Length/Time:	Seven miles; 1 hour round trip
Season:	Fall through spring, weekdays are recommended
Difficulty:	Two stars
Trail Surface:	Wide, dirt roads, 80%; steep, dirt roads (optional), 20%
Trail Grade:	Climb: 500 feet; average grade, 3.0%

General:
There are flat trails for easy riding.   There are also the where you can perform cartwheels, if you so choose! Many of the trails found here were developed for speed while others resemble the dips and turns of a roller coaster.

Logistics:
This area is located south of Chula Vista and east of Imperial Beach. Exit I-805 at Palm Avenue and proceed east (note: this is the Palm Avenue exit that is located south of Chula Vista, not the one in National City). Parking is available at the east end of Palm Avenue, (F, 3).

Miles from Start	Route Directions: 7A - Otay Mesa (Dennery Canyon, or "The Pits")	Miles to End
0.00	From the east end of Palm Avenue, [F,3] turn left (north) immediately and weave your way downhill to the powerline road heading east.	6.5
0.7	Cross under powerlines heading north and south.	5.8
2.2	Arrive at the northeast corner of this area, turn right (south) and head uphill. [D,9] (The longer you wait to head south, the steeper the routes to choose from!)	4.3
2.8	Pass junkyards on the left (said to be the most extensive auto graveyards in the Californias).	3.7
3.4	Turn right heading west on a suitable trail just north of Otay Mesa Road. [J,9]	3.1
4.1	Turn right and follow powerlines heading northwest [J,5] (or you will get stuck on very steep trails and a winding boundary line in the southwest corner of this area.).	2.4
5.3	Head north parallel to the freeway. [I,3]	1.2
6.5	Back to start at I-805 and Palm Avenue.	0.0

OTAY MESA, at the east end of Palm Avenue (San Diego/San Ysidro), is an ancient marine terrace dissected by Dennery Canyon draining north to Otay Valley. Known as "The Pits," it is a natural playground for OHV's. - LL

SAN DIEGO TROLLEY Bike-N-Ride Program is a boon for convenient access for bikers to such tour areas as Otay Mesa, Otay Mountain, (Palm Ave. station shown above), Mission Bay, Rose Canyon, Tecolote Canyon, Balboa Park, and Mission Trails Park. Call MTS 239-2644 for pass information. - LL

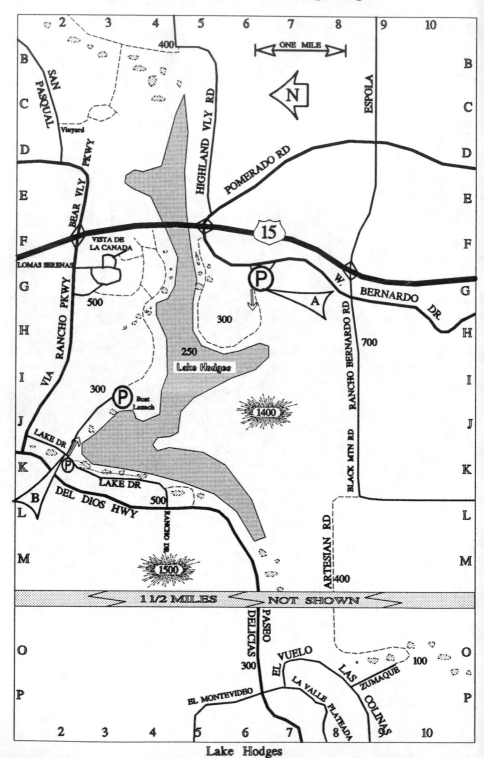

Lake Hodges

Tour No.:   8

Title: Lake Hodges

Overview:
Lake Hodges is a canyon-lake with mountains surrounding most of it. The mountains are scenic, but their near-vertical faces do not permit development of a trail which follows the shoreline all the way around the lake. Therefore, the round trip in this area circumscribes the surrounding large land masses and results in a fairly long ride. There are, however, two sections of trail along the lakeside, each about 3 miles long, which are very colorful. This is especially true of the northern trail, which includes a waterfall.

Trip 8A:	Round Trip - Lake Hodges
Length/Time:	25 miles, 4 hours round trip
Season:	Fall through spring
Difficulty:	Two stars
Trail Surface:	Dirt trails, 20%; dirt roads, 25%; public roads, 55%
Trail Grade:	Climb: 1100 feet; average grade, 1.7%

General:
Although this tour is a "trip around the lake," less than half provides views of the water. The shortest route available actually forms a circle quite a bit larger than Lake Hodges. Due to the mountains in the area, there is a moderate amount of climbing, but the rugged San Diego countryside is gorgeous. The long downhill on Del Dios Highway is fun and has a wide shoulder to ride on.

Logistics:
The area is located near Escondido. Exit I-15 at West Bernardo Drive/Pomerado Road. Head southwest on West Bernardo Drive and at one mile, turn right into the northern-most parking lot of the Rancho Bernardo Community Park. Park near the Senior Center [G,6].

Miles from Start	Route Directions: 8A - Lake Hodges Round Trip	Miles to End
0.00	Head west (stay to the left) on the trail that starts off the edge of the parking lot with a small wooden bridge, right across from the senior center. [G,6]	24.60
0.45	Take the narrow trail towards the left, along the lake.	24.15
1.45	Some shade trees appear. [G,5]	23.15
1.80	Turn left on West Bernardo Drive heading east across I-15.	22.80
2.00	Take I-15 north, bikes are allowed only on shoulder, (and only north of West Bernardo Drive). Cross the lake. [F,5]	22.60
3.00	Take the first exit, Via Rancho Parkway and turn left heading west. [F,3]	21.60
3.40	Turn left and uphill on Lomas Serenas.	21.20
3.75	Turn left on Avienda Amorosa.	20.85
3.95	Turn left on Vista de la Canada.	20.65
4.00	Between the first and second house from the corner, on the right (southwest side) of Vista de la Canada, turn right on what appears to be a driveway. It is the access road to the trail. It is paved and descends sharply for 1/10 mile.	20.60
4.10	Turn right at the bottom of the paved trail onto a wide dirt trail. [F,4]	20.50
4.20	Turn left on the first single track trail, which heads down towards the lake shore.	20.40
4.40	Turn right heading west at the end of the single track on the wide trail along the shore. [G,4]	20.20
4.90	Stream crossing.	19.70
6.80	Arrive at the boat launch parking lot. [I,3] Stay to the right on the road leading to Lake Drive.	17.80
7.90	Turn left on Lake Drive. [K,2] (While you are heading south on Lake Drive there will be some obscure trails through the trees on the left that are interesting to putt around on).	16.70
9.00	(Option: When you get to the point where Lake Drive turns west and uphill (it also turns into Rancho Drive near here), there will be a trail head on the left (east) side of the road with a "San Dieguito River Parks Trail" sign. If you are here on Saturday or Sunday 11 a.m. - 5:30 p.m., you can take a dirt road along the shoreline for another mile and come out on Del Dios Highway and then take a left from there.)	15.60

Miles from Start	Route Directions: 8A - Lake Hodges Round Trip	Miles to End
9.30	Turn left on the wide bike lane of Del Dios Highway and enjoy the downhill. [L,4]	15.30
10.75	Look over your left shoulder, carefully, to see the dam holding back Lake Hodges. [M,6]	13.85
14.40	Turn left at the stop sign, La Valle Plateada (also labeled Montevideo). [P,6]	10.20
14.60	Turn left on El Vuelo (Turns into Las Colinas)	10.00
15.70	Turn left and downhill on Zumaque. [P,9]	8.90
16.20	Pavement ends.	8.40
16.40	Cross the usually dry San Dieguito River. [O,10]	8.20
16.70	Pavement and uphill starts (Artesian Road).	7.90
20.45	Turn left on Black Mountain Road [L,9] (becomes Rancho Bernardo Road).	4.15
22.60	Turn left heading north on West Bernardo Drive. [G,9]	2.00
24.45	Turn left into north parking lot of Rancho Bernardo Community Park. [G,6]	0.15
24.60	Back to start.	0.00

LAKE HODGES is part of the San Dieguito watershed which drains a vast area of central San Diego County. - SB

Trip No. 8B: North Side - Lake Hodges

Length/Time: Eight miles; one-hour two-way trip

Season: Fall through spring

Difficulty: Two stars

Trail Surface: Wide, dirt trails, 80%; single-track and steep trails
                       (optional), 20%

Trail Grade: Climb: 200 feet; average grade, 1.0%

General:
This tour is short, through the off-road trails on the north side of the lake. The north side shows nice vegetation with a trickling stream. For a little extra distance ride over to Lake Drive via the boat launch road, (J, 3). The stretch along Lake Drive from Del Dios Highway to Via Rancho Parkway is scenic.

Logistics:
The area is located near Escondido. Exit I-15 at Via Rancho Parkway and head west. Just before Del Dios Highway, turn left on Lake Drive. A half mile down on the left will be a road to the boat launch. On Wednesdays, Saturdays, or Sundays, drive down that road one mile to a parking lot. Other days, park on Lake Drive and bike around a gate at entrance on Lake Drive [K,2].

Miles from Start	Route Directions: 8B - Lake Hodges North Side	Miles to End
0.0	Head east on road to boat launch from Lake Drive. [K,2] (If it is Wed., Sat., or Sun., you can drive past normally locked gate and park at lot near launching ramps at [I,3]. This 1.1 mile stretch of road is added to trip mileage.	7.6
1.1	Arrive at boat launch parking lot, stay to left, (north) and proceed to east side of lot where wide dirt trail starts and is labeled by a "San Dieguito" sign. [I,3]	6.5
3.0	Stream crossing.	4.6
3.5	Take a single track trail to the left and uphill to the higher ridge trail. [G,4] (There are a few trails that connect to the higher trail, this is the most gradual).	4.1
3.7	Arrive at the higher trail and turn right.	3.9
3.8	On the left will be a paved trail leading upwards to Vista de la Canada. [F,4] This is the official turn-around point for this trip. Return the same way, or better, go explore!	3.8
7.6	Back to start.	0.0

Trip No. 8C: South Side - Lake Hodges

Length/Time: Four miles, 45 minutes two-way trip

Season: Fall through spring

Difficulty: Two stars

Trail Surface: Wide dirt, 90%; difficult trails (optional, 10%)

Trail Grade: Climb: 100 ft.; average grade, 1.0%

General:

This tour is an exploration of trails on the south shore. They vary in complexity and an easy route is always nearby. Often fishermen cast their lines from the shore near I-15.

Logistics:

The area is located near Escondido. Exit I-15 at West Bernardo Drive/Pomerado Road. Head west on West Bernardo Drive and at one mile, turn right into the northern-most parking lot of the Rancho Bernardo Community Park. Park near the Seniors Center [G,6].

Miles from Start	Route Directions: 8C - Lake Hodges South Side	Miles to End
0.00	Head west (stay to the left) on the trail that starts off the edge of the parking lot with a small wooden bridge, right across from the seniors center. [G,6]	3.60
0.45	Take the narrow trail towards the left, along the lake.	3.15
1.45	Some shade trees appear. [G,5]	2.15
1.80	Arrive at West Bernardo Drive. [F,5] This is the official turn-around point for this trip. (Option: instead of returning the same way, you can take West Bernardo Drive south, back to start). This one (1) mile shortcut is not subtracted from trip mileage.	1.80
3.60	Back to start.	0.00

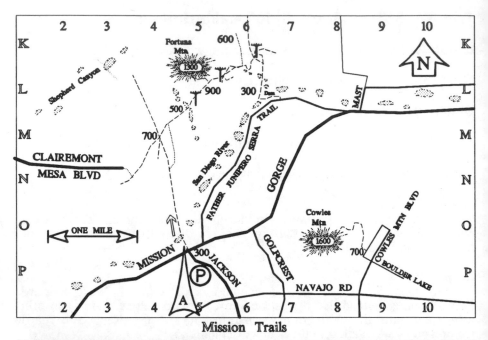

Mission Trails

MISSION TRAILS and the lower San Diego River Canyon is accessible via the dirt trail (no motor vehicles) extension of Jackson Road shown above. The trail drops steeply into the canyon and up in the distance before arcing to the east towards Fortuna Mountain. - BH

Tour No.:   9

Title: Mission Trails Regional Park, Fortuna Mountain

Overview:

Highway 52 has changed this area forever. Blazing right through the middle of Mission Trails Regional Park, it has limited mountain biking to basically one trip centered around the San Diego River and Fortuna Mountain. Some mountain bikers do the 1-1/2 mile climb up the east side of Cowles Mountain also, which is shown on the map, [O-8], but is not described herein. This area was popular with motorcyclists many years ago, and they carved several interesting single-track trails through the area. A few of them are designated trails now, and provide opportunities for the mountain biker to do some exploring off the main-beaten trail described in Trip 9A. There's not a whole lot of shade in this area, so come on a cool day. Many of the trails are steep and/or rocky, so be forewarned!

Trip No. 9A: Mission Trails

Length/Time: Six miles; 1 hour round trip

Season: November to June

Difficulty: Four stars

Trail Surface: Wide, dirt trail, 60%; paved path, (no motorized traffic) 35%; public road, 5%

Trail Grade: Climb: 1100 feet; average grade, 6.6%

General:

This trip involves rugged climbing, especially on the powerline road up towards Fortuna Mountain, and down away from it, on the other side. The area is limited by Route 52, and military land to the north, so stay south of the imaginary line, "[K,2]-[K,10]" on the map, to avoid trespassing. The Old Mission Dam [L,7], built in the early 1800s, is a historic highlight on this trip and Father Junipero Serra Trail, closed to motorized traffic, offers a nice smooth ride along the lush San Diego River.

Logistics:

This tour is near Tierrasanta. Take Mission Gorge Road east from I-8, or west from Route 67, to Jackson Drive. Park on Jackson Drive near Mission Gorge Road (P, 5).

Miles from Start	Route Directions: 9A - Mission Trails	Miles to End
0.00	Pass around gate and head north on the wide trail that starts just east of the intersection of Mission Gorge Road and Jackson Drive. [P,5]	6.32
0.35	Reach bottom of hill and cross the San Diego River. Start of one mile uphill.	5.97
0.94	Pass signed single track trail on the right.	5.38
0.98	Pass another signed single track trail on the right.	5.34
1.18	Arrive at a 5-way intersection at the top of the hill. Take the wide trail to the right that leads downhill. [M,4] (From here you can see the power lines heading east and the trail under them that you will be following towards Fortuna Mountain.)	5.14
1.39	Pass single track trail on the right. (This is the other end of the trail that came in at mile 0.98.)	4.93
1.68	Turn right and downhill at the intersection near the bottom of the valley.	4.64
1.73	Stay to the left on the wide main traveled trail, (just keep in mind that you are heading for the powerline road heading northeast).	4.59
1.84	Stay to the right on the wide main traveled trail.	4.48
2.15	The through-trail is on the north (left) side of the powerlines from here. Steep uphill coming soon.	4.17
2.22	Pass a signed trail on the left.	4.10
2.39	Top of the hill, pass trail to Fortuna Mountain on left. [L,5]	3.93
2.41	Turn left and downhill at 5-way intersection.	3.91
2.94	Bottom of hill, pass signed trail on the left, (Oak Canyon).	3.38
3.03	Pass signed trail on the right, start heading uphill.	3.29
3.07	Stay right on flatter trail.	3.25
3.33	Just before you get to the top of the hill, turn right and down steep rocky trail. [K,6] (From here you can see the San Diego river to the south and your trail leading to it.)	2.99
3.47	Near the bottom of the hill, turn right on a single track trail.	2.85
3.53	Stay right, enjoy smooth downhill.	2.79
3.67	Stay right.	2.65
3.94	Stay right heading uphill out of little valley.	2.38
4.14	Turn left (south) on short trail to river crossing.	2.18
4.16	Cross river on narrow pedestrian bridge. Trail heads east from other side.	2.16
4.29	Check out dam on the left, then continue east.	2.03

Miles from Start	Route Direction: 9A - Mission Trails	Miles to End
4.33	Turn right on trail up to the road, near the picnic tables. Turn right heading west on Father Junipero Serra Trail.	1.99
6.15	Turn right on Mission Gorge Road. [O,5]	0.17
6.32	Back to start.	0.00

MISSION GORGE, looking east from Jackson Drive, is flanked by Fortuna Mountain to the left (north) and Cowles Mountain to the right (south). The patient San Diego River has been more than an erosive match for this slowly rising granitic barrier between Mission Valley and Cajon Valley. - LL

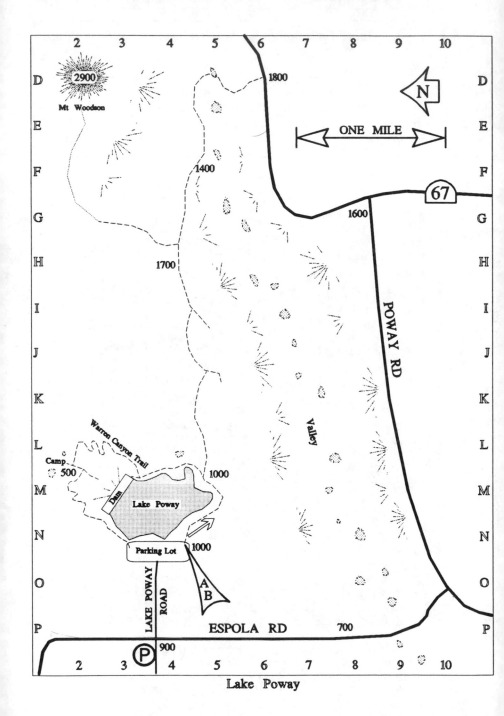

Lake Poway

Tour No.:   10

Title: Lake Poway

Overview:
Surrounded by chaparral coated hills and a few eucalyptus groves, Lake Poway is a beautiful sight. Surprisingly deep for a small lake, (90 feet), the clear water provides a great view of the lake's depths along the shoreline . A city park, Lake Poway is popular with fishermen, and hikers/joggers. The trail around the lake is short but sweet, and includes a one mile section of single-track trail, (Warren Canyon Trail). Trip 10B, which is the trail from the lake to Highway 67, relentlessly steep and overgrown, is for experienced mountain-bikers only. There is a fee to non-Poway residents to park a car near the lake, but it is possible to park on Lake Poway Road, just west of Espola Road, [P,4] and bike in for free.

Trip No. 10A: Around the Lake; Lake Poway

Length/Time: Four miles, 30 minutes round trip

Season: November to May

Difficulty: Two stars

Trail Surface: Wide dirt trails, 80%; single-track trail, 20%; public road, 10%

Trail Grade: Climb: 500 feet; average\grade, 4.5%

General:
This tour consists of a counter-clockwise loop around the lake along with hikers and joggers. The Warren Canyon Trail gets moderately steep in a few spots as it drops to the valley below the lake.

Logistics:
This tour is located in Poway. Exit I-15 at Rancho Bernardo Road and head east. The road becomes Espola Road. Shortly after the big bend south, turn right (west) on Lake Poway Road and park immediately on the side of the road. Fee parking is also available in the park at the east end of Lake Poway Road.

Miles from Start	Route Directions: 10A - Lake Poway Perimeter	Miles to End
0.00	Head east and uphill on Lake Poway Road from the northwest corner of Espola Road and Lake Poway Road. [P,4]	4.22
0.52	Pass through entrance station to the park, then weave your way to the right and go to the southeast corner of the parking lot where the trail starts. [N,4]	3.70
0.80	Enter the trail, stay to the right on the high trail.	3.42
1.53	Pass the trail to Mt. Woodson on the right. [L,4]	2.69
1.89	Turn right and uphill on a narrow trail, (unsigned Warren Canyon Trail) [L,3]	2.33
2.62	Turn left on trail, (right goes to a campground.)	1.60
2.66	Turn right onto a narrow trail again.	1.56
3.24	Stay on the high trail back to the parking lot.	0.98
3.42	Back to parking lot. Head back out the way you came in.	0.80
4.22	Back to start.	0.00

LAKE POWAY offers the easier loop trip around the lake or difficult climb up Mt. Woodson to Hwy. 67. - BH

Trip No. 10B: Lake Poway to Route 67

Length/Time: 12 miles, Two hours round trip

Season: November to May

Difficulty: Five stars

Trail Surface: Public road, 70%; steep eroded trail, 30%

Trail Grade: Climb: 1600 feet; average grade, 5.2%

General:

This trip provides some hard-core mountain biking. The trail is eroded in several spots and can result in unintentional aerial stunts for the less cautious! A picnic table about halfway along this trail is located at an excellent vantage point for viewing the green valley below. You may have to walk about 30% of this trail from the lake to the highway due to the steep grades encountered. A wide shoulder added to Route 67 makes the ride back a relief. A fantastic downhill on Poway Road makes all the hard work pay off!

Logistics:

This tour is located in Poway. Exit I-15 at Rancho Bernardo Road and head east. The road becomes Espola Road. Shortly after the big bend south, turn right (west) on Lake Poway Road and park immediately on the side of the road. Fee parking is also available in the park at the east end of Lake Poway Road.

Miles from Start	Route Directions: 10B - Lake Poway to Route 67 - Round Trip	Miles to End
0.00	Head east and uphill on Lake Poway Road from north-west corner of Espola Road and Lake Poway Road. [P,4]	11.80
0.52	Pass through entrance station to the park then weave your way to the right and go to the southeast corner of the parking lot where the trail starts. [N,4]	11.28
0.80	Enter the trail, stay to the right on the high trail.	11.00
1.53	Turn right and uphill on the trail to Mt. Woodson. Signed by a bulletin board and a post with a horseshoe/foot stamped in it. [L,4]	10.27
1.87	Stay left at the 3-way intersection. [J,4]	9.93
2.34	Stay left at the 3-way intersection. [I,4]	9.46
2.69	Reach a high point in this trip.	9.11
2.73	Pass turn off to Mt. Woodson on the left, signed by post with horseshoe/foot and "Poway" stamped in it. [G,4]	9.07

Miles from Start	Trip No. 10B - Lake Poway to Route 67	Miles to End
3.41	Picnic table.	8.39
4.55	Turn right on Route 67. [D,6]	7.25
6.30	Turn right on Poway Road, awesome downhill next! [F,8]	5.50
8.95	Turn right on Espola Road. [O,10]	2.85
11.77	Turn left on Lake Poway Road. [P,4]	0.03
11.80	Back to start.	0.00

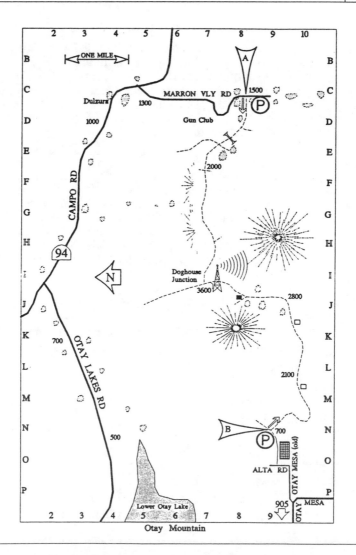

Tour No.:　　11

Title:　　Otay Mountain

Overview:
The Otay Mountain Truck Trail is a rough, dirt road that rises to the mountain top from the foothills on the east and west sides. It serves as access to the antenna installation at Doghouse Junction, which in the past was closed to public access. Otay's summit is one of the higher points in the county that is relatively close to the ocean. Needless to say, from the summit you can enjoy a spectacular view of our city. The mountain is mostly covered with chaparral and shade is sparse around midday. An early or late departure will provide some slanted shadows to rest in. The elevation and winds at the summit usually reduce the temperature slightly. Stamina and low gears are a must for the seven mile uphills on either side of the mountain. This is especially true on the steeper west side. During the long downhill return, stop occasionally to pry your hands from the levers and cool your brakes.

Trip No. 11A:　　East Side, Otay Mountain

Length/Time:　　14 miles, 1-1/2 hours round trip

Season:　　November to May

Difficulty:　　Three stars

Trail Surface:　　Moderately inclined dirt road, 100%

Trail Grade:　　Climb: 2100 feet; average grade 5.9%

General:
This is the milder of the two sides from which to climb. The drive out on Highway 94 (from San Diego) is a twisting, but scenic, route.

Logistics:
This tour starts southeast of Dulzura. Take Highway 94 (Campo Road) east and turn right onto Marron Valley Road, (C, 5). Pass the Gun Club and an open gate, and the dirt road will wind around and down to a wooded area. The trail starts off to the right and there are no signs or gates to label this entry. Park in this area, (C,8).

Miles from Start	Route Directions: 11A - Otay Mountain East Side	Miles to End
0.00	Head west and uphill on Otay Mountain Truck Trail from Marron Valley Road. [C,8]	13.58
0.68	Pass trail on the left.	12.90
1.12	Pass through gate, (keep closed).	12.46
1.26	Stay on the middle fork, (main traveled) at four-way intersection. [E,7]	12.32
2.13	Pass through intersection.	11.45
4.51	Pass trail on the left.	9.07
5.92	Turn left at intersection, (Doghouse Junction). [I,7]	7.66
6.50	Turn right on paved uphill road to towers.	7.08
6.79	Arrive at top of mountain. This is designated turn-around point for this trip. [I,8]	6.79
13.58	Back to start.	0.00

OTAY MOUNTAIN (west side) trailhead is marked by an abandoned fire engine just east of the Donohue Correctional Facility. The dirt road climbs steadily upslope and to right in this view looking east. - LL

Trip No. 11B: West Side, Otay Mountain

Length/Time: 14 miles, two hours, two-way trip

Season: November to May

Difficulty: Three stars

Trail Surface: Moderate inclines, dirt road, 100%

Trail Grade: Climb: 2800 feet; average grade, 7.5%

General:

This tour provides a little more climbing than the east approach. A view of the city slowly unfolds as you gain altitude.

Logistics

The area is located east of San Ysidro. Take Freeway 905 east which, as of this writing, turns into Otay Mesa Road. When Otay Mesa Road is just about to bend south into Mexico, [P, 10], take the old Otay Mesa Road off to the left at the bend. This continues east and then swings north to the new State Prison and becomes Alta Road. Just past the left turn to Donohue Correctional Facility, turn right (east) towards the old Kuebler Ranch [O, 9] in a grove of trees. Pass left around the ranch buildings and park behind (east) uphill of them near power lines.

Miles from Start	Route Directions: 11B - Otay Mountain West Side	Miles to End
0.00	Head east/southeast and uphill on Otay Mountain Truck Trail after you make it past the buildings and the piled-up junk. [N,9]	14.16
2.13	Pass landing pad. [L,10]	12.03
5.43	Pass landing pad. [J,10]	8.73
5.92	Take fork to the right at cement bunker. [J,8]	5.92
6.79	Turn left and uphill on paved road to the towers. [I,7]	7.37
7.08	Arrive at top of mountain. This is the designated turn-around point for this trip.	7.08
14.16	Back to start.	0.00

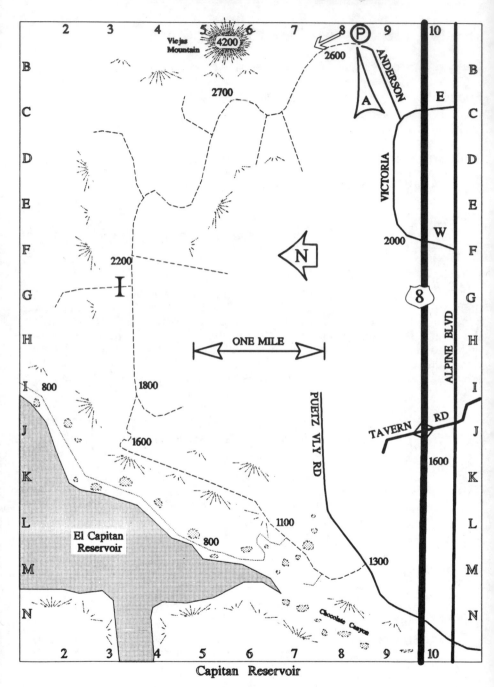

Capitan Reservoir

Tour No.:   12

Title: Alpine to El Capitan Reservoir

Overview:

This tour is under an hour by auto from the ocean on I-8. El Capitan is one of the largest reservoirs in our county. Although popular with a large number of San Diego mountain bikers, it was first shown to me by an Alpine resident as a two-day trip. We crossed north under I-8 onto Peutz Valley Road from Alpine Boulevard (N,10) to the Peutz Valley Road trailhead (L, 7) which is almost invisible from the road. We then proceeded down to the trail at the waterline and continued to the reservoir's north end (see the Cleveland National Forest map for more of this trail). We camped that night near the junction of Cedar Creek and the San Diego River. The next day took us uphill to Julian, then south on Highway 79 through the Cuyamacas. Our "number two" car was parked near I-8 where we ended our trip.

Although that trip was a bit much, another one we took counterclockwise on the Anderson Truck Trail and Peutz Valley Road through Alpine, was enjoyable and much shorter. This trip started from Point B on our map (J,4), on Anderson Truck Trail. It then proceeded southwest down the trail to Puetz Valley Road, then east up through Alpine on Alpine Boulevard, left on West Victoria, left on Anderson and back down the trail to the starting point (J,4). Unfortunately, a visit to the county assessor's office uncovered the fact that a small piece of land near the waterfall (M, 7) is privately owned. (This is surprising due to the absence of any signs or fences, and it means that riders should turn around at this mysterious property line.).

Trip No. 12A: Anderson Truck Trail

Length/Time: 12 miles, 3 hours two-way trip

Season: Fall to spring

Difficulty: Three stars

Trail Surface: Graded dirt road, 70%; eroded dirt road, 20%; eroded single-track (optional), 10%

Trail Grade: Climb: 1700 feet; average grade, 5.3%

General:

This is a dirt road that starts in Alpine and ends near the reservoir. The road gets progressively more eroded from east to west. This ride is about as close to an airplane ride that a mountain bike can get! It consists mostly of coasting one way (towards the lake) and, from (J, 3) to (L, 7) there is as much as a 1000 foot drop-off down to the lake surface below. Combine this aerial view with the speed of the downhill, and you're flying!

Logistics:

This tour starts in Alpine. Exit I-8 at Tavern Road south. Turn left on Alpine Boulevard through town, left on West Victoria, then left on Anderson. Follow Anderson to the end. At the point where it becomes a dirt road, park at the roadside in a pullout (B, 8), Point A on the map. This is USFS 15s30.

Miles from Start	Route Directions: 12A - Alpine to El Capitan Reservoir via Anderson Truck Trail	Miles to End
0.00	Head northwest on Anderson Truck Trail from north end of Anderson Road where pavement ends. [B,8], (Point A).	12.10
0.78	Pass a driveway on the left.	11.32
0.97	Pass a driveway on the left.	11.13
1.07	Pass Rainbow Farms on the left. [C,7]	11.03
1.26	Pass a road on the right.	10.84
1.46	Take fork to the left, (right goes into private property just around the bend).	10.64
2.23	Pass a driveway on the right.	9.87
2.33	Pass a driveway on the right (Anderson Valley).	9.77
2.62	Take fork to the right. [I,4]	9.48
3.69	Pass a road on the left.	8.41
3.78	Go around ancient road closed sign [J,4], (Point B).	8.32
3.98	Wide road ends, it is downhill and single track all the way to the turn-around point!	8.12
5.82	Pass turn-off on the right to the waterline trail. [L,7] A boulder with graffiti is near the trailhead. The trail is very overgrown but goes all the way to the north end of the reservoir although it does require bushwhacking just about the time you reach Indian land. (See Cleveland National Forest map).	7.08
6.05	Reach waterfall on the left, (usually dry). This is the designated turn-around point for this trip because this is near where a (unsigned) private inholding is.	6.05
12.10	Back to start.	0.00

ANDERSON TRUCK TRAIL, north from Alpine, links several ranches and the Capitan Grande Indian Reservation in Cleveland National Forest with sweeping vistas and a plunging descent to the reservoir. - LL

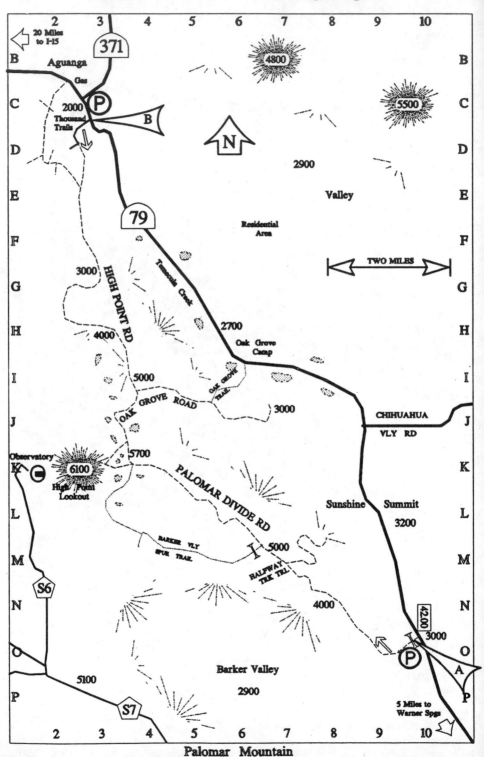

Palomar Mountain

Tour No.:   13

Title: Palomar Mountain

Overview:

Otay Mountain, in San Diego's backyard, and Palomar's east side are very similar. These are BIG mountains with lots of steady climbing on chaparral covered slopes - meaning: there is not much shade. The road, a moderately steep grade all the way to the summit, was constructed with function more than recreation in mind. But, this mountain is even bigger than Otay with a view radius of over 150 miles from the lookout. Groves of pines and oaks occur above 5000 feet. The trail, like Otay's, is open to highway-legal vehicles, but there is not much of this traffic. The tour is a two-hour drive from downtown San Diego.

Trip No. 13A: East Divide, Palomar Mountain

Length/Time: 25 miles, 4 hours to lookout and back

Season: Winter

Difficulty: Two stars

Trail Surface: Graded dirt road, 100%

Trail Grade: Climb: 3100 feet; average grade, 4.7%

General:

The most dramatic views occur on this side of the mountain. Around the 4000 foot mark the valley below opens up wide and far. It appears lifeless until someone drives through. Then a wall of dust rises, curling like smoke. Is this the origin of "blazing a trail?" A few times during the ascent, a view of the observatory pokes through. At the intersection with the road to High Point (K, 4), some shade finally appears in coniferous and deciduous forms.

Logistics:

The trip area begins five miles north of Warner Springs. The trail starts just south of the 42.00 mile marker on Highway 79. Park anywhere near the trailhead [O, 9].

Miles from Start	Route Directions: 13A - East Divide, Palomar Mountain	Miles to End
0.00	Head west and uphill on Palomar Divide Road (labeled 9S07) from Highway 79. [O,10]	24.83
1.75	Cross Cleveland National Forest boundary. [O,9]	23.08
3.30	Pass through open gate.	21.53
5.63	Pass landing pad.	19.20
6.98	Pass Halfway Trail on the right. [M,7]	17.85
7.66	Pass Barker Valley Spur Trail on the left. [L,6]	17.17
11.16	Pass the other end of the Barker Valley Spur Trail. [K,4]	13.67
11.25	Turn left on trail in tunnel of trees. [K,4]	13.58
11.35	Pass trail on the right.	13.48
11.64	Turn left on trail.	13.19
12.13	Turn left on trail to High Point. [K,3]	12.70
12.42	Arrive at top of mountain. This is the designated turn-around point for this trip. Return the same way you came up.	12.42
24.83	Back to start.	0.00

Trip No. 13B: Round Trip, East Side, Palomar Mountain

Length/Time: 34 miles, five hours round trip

Season: Winter

Difficulty: Two stars

Trail Surface: Graded dirt road, 50%; highway 79, 50%

Trail Grade: Climb: 4000 feet; average grade, 4.4%

General:
Most shade is along the highway where the creek is. There is not much of a shoulder along Highway 79, which could pose a problem if the traffic is heavy. However, the traffic is light during the week.

Logistics:
The trip area begins five miles north of Warner Springs. The trail starts just south of the 42.00 mile marker on Highway 79. Park anywhere near the trailhead [O, 9].

Miles to End	Route Directions: 13B - Round Trip, Palomar Mountain	Miles from Start
0.00	Head west and uphill on Palomar Divide Road (labeled 9S07) from Highway 79. [O,10]	33.95
1.75	Cross Cleveland National Forest boundary. [O,9]	32.20
3.30	Pass through open gate.	30.65
5.63	Pass landing pad.	28.32
6.98	Pass Halfway Trail on the right. [M,7]	26.97
7.66	Pass Barker Valley Spur Trail on the left. [L,6]	26.29
10.83	Pass the other end of the Barker Valley Spur Trail. [K,4]	23.12
11.25	Stay to the right on Palomar Divide Road. [K,4] (Option: At this point you could turn left and by taking the next three left turns, arrive at High Point Lookout. See Trip 13A above. This 2.4 mile detour not added to trip mileage).	22.70
11.45	Turn right on Oak Grove Road, [K,4], USFS 9s09.	22.50
13.10	Turn left on High Point Road. [I,4] (Option: It is possible to alter the round trip by heading down to Highway 79 on Oak Grove Road. The only problem is that it ends in private property, so to avoid trespassing, you must take a left on a very difficult single track trail at [J,5] down on Oak Grove Trail. This altered route not reflected in trip mileage).	20.85
20.86	Pass road on the left, [E,3], USFS 8s05.	13.09
21.24	Stay on main traveled trail.	12.71
21.34	Trail turns into the paved driveway of Thousand Trails campground. Continue north then east back to the highway. [D,2]	12.61
21.73	Turn right on Highway 79 heading southeast. [D,3]	12.22
23.47	Cross San Diego County line.	10.48
26.77	Oak Grove. [H,6]	7.18
30.17	Pass Chihuahua Valley Road on the left. [J,9]	3.78
33.85	Turn right on Palomar Divide Road just south of mile marker "42".	0.10
33.95	Back to start.	0.00

Trip No. 13C: North Side, Palomar Mountain

Length/Time: 24 miles, three hours to lookout and back

Season: Winter to early summer

Difficulty: Two stars

Trail Surface: Graded dirt road, 100%

Trail Grade: Climb: 4100 feet; average grade, 6.4%

General:
The hills and grades encountered on this trip in the Temecula watershed are somewhat steeper than those of Trip 14A. Like the previous two trips, it is almost entirely within the Cleveland National Forest. It climbs to San Diego County's third highest peak.

Logistics:
This trip starts near Aguanga just over the boundary into Riverside County. Park near the Highways 79 and 371 intersection, [C, 3].

Miles from Start	Route Directions: 13C - North Side, Palomar Mountain	Miles to End
0.00	Head west on the paved driveway to Thousand Trails campground (also labeled 8s05) elev. 1,900 ft.. [C,3]	24.24
0.39	When the driveway makes a sharp right turn, stay straight ahead onto the dirt High Point Road [D,2] Point B.	23.85
0.45	Stay on the main traveled trail.	23.79
0.87	Pass trail on the right.	23.37
8.63	Turn right on Oak Grove Road [I,4] 9s09.	15.61
10.28	Turn right on road (Palomar Divide Road to the left) and stay on main traveled trail [J/K,3.5] 9s07.	13.96
11.83	Turn left on road to High Point, elev. 6,140 ft.	12.41
12.12	Arrive at top of mountain. This is the official turn-around point for this trip. Return the same way you came up.	12.12
24.24	Back to start at Thousand Trails near Aguanga.	0.00

CAREFUL CROSS CHECKING between maps and guidebook is essential to safety in the remote backcountry. - DEL

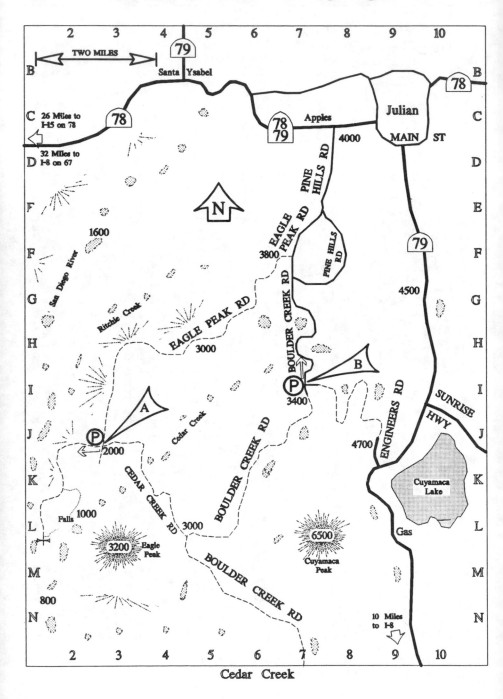

Cedar Creek

Tour No.:   14

Title: Cedar Creek, Eagle Peak

Overview:
This tour is in an area that doesn't get much traffic even though it is in beautiful mountain terrain between Julian and the Cuyamacas. The higher elevations are in pleasant forest land, and as elevation decreases, the mountain gradually becomes bald, losing the larger trees. In the chaparral covered area are dramatic, sheer drop-offs to Ritchie Creek below. This is definitely a worthwhile area to tour even if you only take the trip from Cuyamaca Lake over Engineers Road to Julian, to get some apple cider!

Trip No. 14A: Cedar Creek Falls

Length/Time: Six miles, one hour two-way trip

Season: Fall through spring

Difficulty: Three stars

Trail Surface: Eroded dirt, 80%; rock, 15%; carry, 5%

Trail Grade: Climb: 1200 feet, average grade, 7.3% elevation

General:
This short trip will take you to one of the tallest waterfalls in the county (90 feet tall). From the starting point, it is almost completely downhill to the falls, on a narrow eroded trail. The turn-off to the top of the falls, [K,2], starts as a short, steep, and rocky trail over a low saddle, then, just as steeply, down to Cedar Creek and the falls. The main trail leads to the bottom of the falls, but unfortunately passes through a stretch of government land, the boundary of which is the 995 foot elevation level. Although the boundary is marked with a fence, a bypass trail sort-of-avoiding the 995 foot contour line, has been worn in by visitors to the area. The only strictly legal route is a "goat trail" heading almost vertically down from the top of the falls.

Logistics:
This tour area is on the western slopes of the mountain range between Julian and Cuyamaca. Exit I-8 at Highway 79 and proceed north. Turn left on USFS 13s03, Engineers Road, [K, 9] at Lake Cuyamaca. The road becomes dirt, but becomes pavement again near the forest station [I, 7]. Turn right on Boulder Creek Road, USFS 13s08, proceed to Eagle Peak Road and turn left, USFS 13s06[(F, 7]. On dirt once again, mostly downhill, you can drive all the way down to the four-way intersection at [J, 3]. If the road is too steep, there is also parking at the cattle crossing, about a half mile before four-way crossing, [I, 3].

Miles from Start	Route Directions: 14A - Cedar Creek Falls	Miles to End
0.0	Head west and downhill on the trail from the four way intersection. [J,3]	6.2
1.5	Turn left on steep uphill, narrow eroded trail with no other sign other than some rocks that are usually piled-up near its base. [K,2] (This trail leads to top of Cedar Creek Falls)	4.7
1.6	Reach a high point and view of Cedar Creek below and to the east.	4.6
1.8	Pass trail on the left.	4.4
2.0	Reach end of trail and top of the falls. You will have to carry your bike 100ft. over the last stretch of trail that is basically boulder-hopping. Head back up the same trail you just came in on.	4.2
2.5	Back to the main trail. Turn left heading downhill to see the pool at the bottom of the falls.	3.7
3.2	When you see the gates ending the trail, look for a side trail to the left that will skirt along the fence and keep you from trespassing. Once you go down a little hill, turn left on the wide trail heading north. [L/M,2]	3.0
3.6	Arrive at the bottom of the falls. Again you must boulder-hop with your bike on your shoulder to reach the edge of the pool. This is the designated turn-around point for this trip. Head back the way you came, it is all uphill!	2.6
6.2	Back to start.	0.0

EQUESTRIANS share many favored dirt roads and trails in the Cuyamacas with mountain bikers. Always yield right-of-way to horses. - LL

Trip No. 14B: Cedar Creek, Eagle Creek

Length/Time: 19 miles, three hours round trip

Season: Fall through spring

Difficulty: Four stars

Trail Surface: Graded dirt, 60%; exposed rocks, 20%; paved with very light traffic, 20%

Trail Grade: Climb: 2000 feet, average grade, 4.1%

General:

This trip starts with an easy run on pavement through beautiful woods. After a left turn on the graded-dirt Eagle Peak Road, it is mostly downhill for the next seven miles. Beware, at [H,3] there are usually two dogs that wait for passersby to chase. The best defense with them is, as usual with dogs, stop, get off and walk your bike. They no longer see you as a target then. After turning left at the four-way intersection, [J,3], the road is eroded. This is the best part of the trip as you travel through strips of riparian vegetation with trickling streams. There are some steep climbs on Cedar Creek Road and a stop under a shady tree will be pleasurable. After turning left on the graded-dirt Boulder Creek Road, it is a steady grind uphill back to start.

Logistics:

Exit I-8 at Highway 79 and proceed north to Engineers Road at Lake Cuyamaca. Park at the Pine Hills Fire Station at the intersection of Engineers Road and Boulder Creek Road, (J, 9).

Miles from Start	Route Directions: 14B - Eagle Peak, Cedar and Boulder Creek.	Miles to End
0.00	Head north on the paved Boulder Creek Road from the fire station, [I,7], USFS 13s08.	18.72
2.23	Pass scout camp on the left.	16.49
2.81	Turn left on Pine Hills Road, [G,7], USFS 13s07	15.91
3.10	Turn left,downhill on Eagle Peak Road, 13s06 (dirt). [F,7]	15.62
9.22	Dogs will usually chase you for about 1/2 a mile here. Use your bike pump or mace to threaten them. You may have to walk until they lose interest in you. [I,3]	9.50
10.48	Turn left and downhill heading east on the eroded trail at the four-way intersection. This is the Cedar Creek Road 13s11, [J,3]. (Option: At this point you could tack on trip 14A to Cedar Falls. This 6.2 mile detour not added to trip mileage.)	8.24

Miles from Start	Trip No. 14B - Eagle Peak, Cedar and Boulder Creek	Miles to End
11.35	Pass trail on the right. [J,4]	7.37
13.97	Turn left heading east and uphill on wide and maintained Boulder Creek Road, 13s08, [L,5]	4.75
18.72	Back to start.	0.00

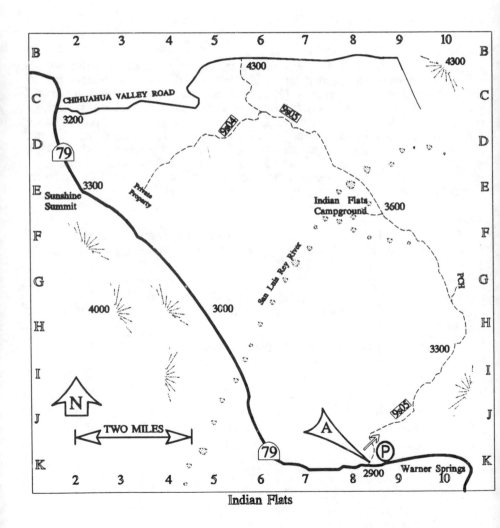

Indian Flats

Tour No.: 15

Title: Indian Flats

Overview:
This tour is a loop through the valley just east of Palomar Mountain on a mix of paved and dirt road roads. It crosses the fertile San Luis Rey river valley twice, and offers views of pine topped, boulder-covered mountains.

Trip No. 15A: **Indian Flats, San Luis Rey River Loop**

Length/Time: 24 miles, three hours round trip

Season: Fall through spring

Difficulty: Two stars

Trail Surface: Decayed paved road (very light traffic), 20%; Forest Service dirt road, 20%; public roads, 60%

Trail Grade: Climb: 2000 feet; average grade, 3.2%

General:
This trip will take you past Indian Flats Campground on the San Luis Rey River - a shady spot to stop and check out the view. There is a fast downhill on Chihuahua Valley Road (light traffic with average one-foot shoulder). The ride on Highway 79 (moderate traffic, usually no shoulder) is almost flat.

Logistics:
Take Highway 79, 1-1/2 miles west of Warner Springs. A Forest Service road will be on the right with a clearing large enough to park a few cars.

Miles from Start	Route Directions: 15A - Indian Flats	Miles to End
0.00	Head north on Indian Flats Road (labeled Forest Service 9s05) from Highway 79. [K,8]	23.75
1.46	Cleveland National Forest boundary.	22.29
4.37	Pass access road to Pacific Crest Trail on the right. [G,10] (Off-limits to mountain bikes.)	19.38
6.11	Pass Indian Flats Campground on the left. [E,9]	17.64
7.76	Cleveland National Forest Boundary.	16.00

Miles from Start	Route Directions: 15A - Indian Flats	Miles to End
9.60	Turn right heading north. [C,6] (Left is Forest Service road 9s04.)	14.15
10.55	Turn left heading west on Chihuahua Valley Road.	13.20
14.65	Turn left heading south on Highway 79. [C,2] 9.10	
23.75	Back to start.	0.00

PRUDENT BACKCOUNTRY TRAVELERS anticipate and are properly equipped to cope with natural, human, and mechanical hazards. - LL

MINIMUM SAFETY EQUIPMENT includes ample water supply (and frequent drinking), helmet, spare tube(s), and sun protection. - LL

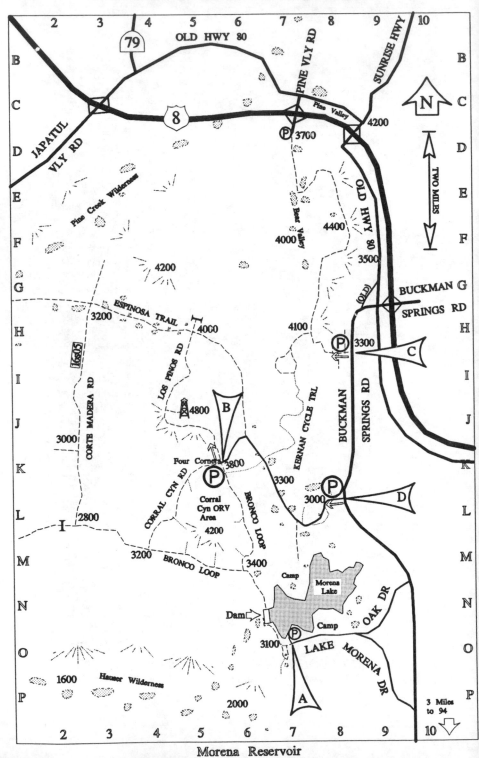

Morena Reservoir

Tour No.: 16

Title: Morena Lake, Corral Canyon and Bear Valley

Overview:

This tour area is between Pine Valley and Morena Village, about 80 miles from the coast on Interstate 8. Between the three trips described below, there is a wide range of mountain biking adventures possible -- the very flat and short 16A; the long and rugged 16B; and the paved (light traffic) and wooded 16C.

Trip No. 16A: Morena Lake, South Side

Length/Time: Four miles, one-hour two-way trip

Season: October to June; weekdays recommended

Difficulty: One star

Trail Surface: Wide, dirt road, 100%

Trail Grade: Climb: 200 feet; average grade, 1.7%

General:

This trip provides a simple ride on a smooth dirt trail, with an optional visit to a primitive wooded campsite. There is a fairly large and popular park/campground on the south side of the lake, which provides an excellent spot to picnic. There is a fee to park a car in the campground, but it is possible to leave the car somewhere outside and bike in for free.

Logistics:

The area is located 30 miles east of Alpine by road. Exit I-8 at Buckman Springs Road and head south. Turn right at Oak Drive, (following signs to Morena Lake), and as you drive through Morena Village towards the lake, the road goes straight into the campgrounds. Take the main road as far west as it will go, (stay to the left), and just as the road makes its last bend towards the lake and a boat launch, you will see the trail on the left. A cable is stretched across its entrance. Park anywhere in the area. There are some nice spots right on the water.

Miles from Start	Route Directions: 16A - Morena Lake South Side	Miles to End
0.00	Head west on the wide dirt trail towards the dam. [O,7]	4.30
1.03	Pass trail on the left that goes to a tin barn.	3.27
1.10	Turn left on trail heading south and slightly uphill to a primitive campground.	3.20
1.65	South end of the campground, stay right and loop back on the other side heading north.	2.65
2.16	Back to main trail to dam, turn left. [O,6.5]	2.14
2.58	Arrive at gate, and pump house. This is the designated turn-around point for this trip. [N,6] Although often left wide open, "no trespassing" is posted on the gate across trail to dam. If you climb down on the big rocks below the pump house you can catch a glimpse of the dam. (It is 0.11 miles from the gate to the dam.)	1.72
4.30	Back to start.	0.00

Trip No. 16B: Los Pinos Lookout, Espinosa Trail, and Corral Canyon

Length/Time: 16 miles; two hours for perimeter round trip

Season: October to June, weekdays recommended

Difficulty: Four stars

Trail Surface: Wide, rough, and steep, dirt trail, 75%; wide, moderately-eroded, dirt trail, 25%

Trail Grade: Climb: 2300 feet; average grade, 5.4%

General:
The area in the vicinity of (L, 6), with its triangle of trails, is one in which anyone may ride the countryside with any type of motorized vehicle - legally. Outside of the Off-Road Vehicle (O.R.V.) area, the law requires that vehicles must stay on existing trails. There is the danger of slow mountain bicyclists becoming mixed with the fast motorized crowd. The danger is somewhat lessened by the noise heard as vehicles approach. However, bikers should proceed with caution. The area is covered with chaparral. Sweeping views of the surrounding countryside may be seen from the lookout. The immediate area around the Corral Canyon O.R.V. area gets noisy and dusty, especially on weekends. The outlying areas get much less traffic.

Logistics:

This area is located 20 miles east of Alpine by road. Exit I-8 at Buckman Springs, and head south. At approximately Mile Marker 6.5 there will be a signed turn-off on the right to "Corral Canyon O.R.V. Area." Take that west until you reach the Four Corners parking lot [K, 5].

Miles from Start	Route Directions: 16B - Corral Canyon, Espinosa Trail	Miles to End
0.00	Head north and uphill on Los Pinos Road [K,5] 16s17.	16.12
2.23	Pass turn-off to lookout tower on right, (interesting detour). [J,4] The worst of the uphill is over, but now the bumps start!	13.89
3.10	Pass Spur Meadow Road on the left. [I,5]	13.02
3.88	Turn left on the unsigned Espinosa Trail. [H,5] This is the start of the most rugged section of the trip, although mostly downhill.	12.24
4.66	Pass water tanks on the left.	11.46
6.11	Pass trail on the left. [H,4]	10.01
6.40	Pass trail sign on left, (facing the other way, warning of the brutal trail you just took)!	9.72
6.79	Pass trail on the right. Turn south onto Corte Madera Road, [G,3], USFS 16s05.	9.33
7.28	Pass through gate.	8.84
9.02	Pass trail on the right [K,3] to Skye Valley.	7.10
10.19	Stay to the right, many trails veer off to the left, most zig-zagging back to the main trail.	5.93
10.57	Stay on trail along fence heading south. When fence comes to a corner and turns to the west (right), head east (left) on the trail [L/M,2.5] 17s06, elev. 2,879 ft.	5.55
11.93	Pass trail on the right [M,3] to Stokes Valley.	4.19
12.32	Turn left on Corral Canyon Road [M,4] 17s04. This major intersection gives you the option of taking the slightly milder Bronco Loop to the right. It is 2 additional miles back to start on Bronco Loop, 17s17. These extra 2 miles not added to trip mileage.	3.80
13.29	Pass Gunslinger on the right [L,5].	2.83
14.94	Pass Corral Canyon campground on the right [K,5].	1.18
16.12	Back to start at Four Corners.	0.00

Trip No. 16C: Bear Valley - Pine Valley Loop

Length/Time: 15 miles; two hours round trip

Season: October to June, weekdays recommended

Difficulty: Four stars

Trail Surface: Wide, eroded, dirt trail, 60%, public road, 40%

Trail Grade: Climb: 1800 feet; average grade, 4.7%

General:

The occasionally steep and rocky trail of this tour is open to 4 x 4's and is connected to the Corral Canyon O.R.V. area by way of the Kernan Cycle Trail, [J, 7]. The northern section of Bear Valley is open for target practice. It provides an opportunity to strap on a six-shooter, if you so wish!

Logistics:

Trip area is located southeast of Pine Valley. Exit I-8 at Buckman Springs Road. Proceed southwest one mile to point just south of Mile Marker 9. A gate at trailhead. Cleveland National Forest signs posted just beyond, [H, 9].

Miles from Start	Route Directions: 16C - Bear Valley Loop	Miles to End
0.00	Head west and uphill on the main trail, [H,8], 16s12.	14.55
1.65	Pass signed Kernan Cycle Trail on the left.	12.90
2.04	Pass landing pad on the right.	12.51
2.13	Pass trail on the right.	12.42
2.15	Enter shooting area.	12.40
2.33	Leave shooting area.	12.22
4.46	Pass trail on the left.	10.09
6.40	Enter shooting area.	8.15
7.18	Leave shooting area.	7.37
7.95	Back to pavement, continue north,Pine Valley Road. [C,7]	6.60
8.45	Right on Old Highway 80, in Pine Valley, east and climbing.	6.10
9.89	Right heading south and downhill, Sunrise Highway, at Laguna Summit (turns back into Hwy 80). Cross I-8. [D,9]	4.66
13.10	Turn right on Old Buckman Springs Road. [G,9]	1.45
13.97	Turn right on Buckman Springs Road.	0.58
14.45	Turn right heading west off of Buckman Springs road back to start. [H,8]	0.10
14.55	Back to start.	0.00

*BEAR VALLEY, MORENA LAKE, AND CORRAL CANYON area
alternates between open meadows, pine forests, and oak groves. Numerous
dirt roads and trails crisscross the area. - DEL*

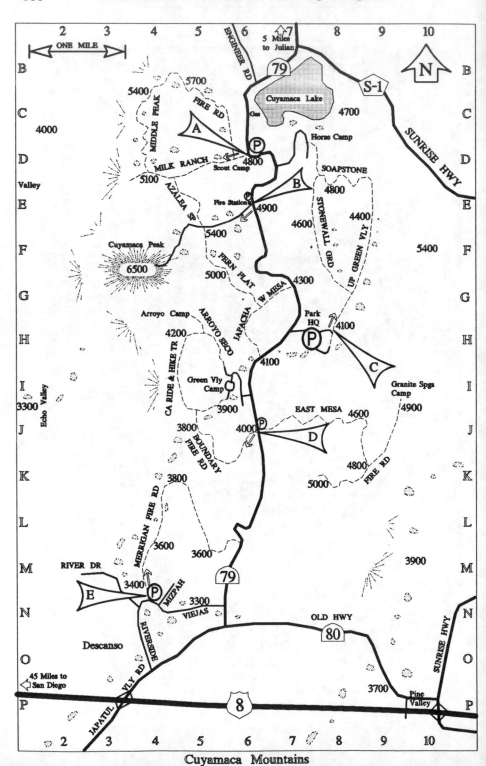

Cuyamaca Mountains

Tour No.: 17

Title: Cuyamaca Mountains

Overview:

This tour area is 1-1/2 hours by auto from the ocean on I-8. "One minute you're riding a wave at O.B. and ninety minutes later you're in a dense forest of pines at an elevation of over one mile above sea level!" So says a promotion for San Diego with her awesome diversity. This is the most popular mountain area in our county, and for a good reason - this area is fantastic! About one half of the approximately 100 miles of trails in the Cuyamacas are open to mountain bikers. Only the trails that are open to mountain biking are shown on the map. Obviously there are many more routes possible than the ones described below. Be sure to get Harrison's Trail Map of Cuyamaca State Park. This excellent topographic map of the area is available at the Park Headquarters (H, 7) for a small fee and most county bookstores. Headquarters is open from 8:00 a.m. to 5:00 p.m., Monday through Friday. There is a 15 mph speed limit for mountain bikes in the park, and it's a good idea. This is the area where you will contact and must defer to equestrians and hikers. These mountainous trails, with their thin air and steep grades, are something you may "graduate to" after you have developed crash experience, extra lung stamina and graceful techniques of quietly yielding to skittish horses and riders!

Trip No. 17A: Middle Peak, Cuyamaca Mountains

Length/Time: Six miles; 1.5 hours round trip

Season: Fall, spring; weekdays recommended

Difficulty: Three stars

Trail Surface: Fire road, 100%

Trail Grade: Climb: 1200 feet; average grade, 7.3%

General:

This area is the enchanted forest of San Diego County - for mountain bikers, that is. There are trees here that simulate the Giant Sequoia of Northern California - in looks, that is - not quite in size! The tour features tunnels of pine, oak, and cedar, resulting in a trip that may shock anyone caught in city-life doldrums!

Logistics:

This trip is in the vicinity of Cuyamaca Lake. The trail begins near the Boy Scout Camp (Hual-Cu-Cuish) entrance. Park at the Highway 79 lot, [D, 6].

Miles from Start	Route Directions: 17A - Middle Peak, Cuyamaca Mountains	Miles to End
0.00	Pass through gate signed "To forest service lands," and head west on Milk Ranch Road. [D,6]	6.22
0.15	Pass Middle Peak Fire Road on the right.	6.07
1.61	Pass trail to Azalea Spring on left.	4.61
1.98	Turn right on Middle Peak Fire Road and go around gate to north. [D,4]	4.24
5.01	Turn left on Middle Peak Fire Road. (Sign says "To Hwy 79"). [C,5]	1.21
5.56	Pass Sugar Pine Fire Road on left.	0.66
6.07	Turn left on Milk Ranch Road. [D,6]	0.15
6.22	Back to entrance gate.	0.00

Trip No. 17B: Cuyamaca Peak

Length/Time: Six miles; one hour to top and down

Season: Fall, spring; weekdays recommended

Difficulty: Two stars

Trail Surface: Paved, steep road, no cars, 100%

Trail Grade: Climb: 1600 feet, average grade, 11%

General:
This is a trip for those tired of bumps, but equipped with the gearing to enjoy a steep climb. This paved course takes you directly to a summit of our county, with the possibility of an airborne descent going down! Views are limited only by air clarity and the curvature of the earth.

Logistics:
The trailhead is located just south of the Interpretive Center (E, 6). Parking is available at the day-use lot in the Paso Picacho Picnic Area (D, 6) for a $3.00 fee. The nearest usable roadside lot is one mile north on Highway 79.

Miles from Start	Route Directions: 17B - Cuyamaca Peak	Miles to End
0.00	Head west and uphill, around the fire station, on the paved Cuyamaca Peak Fire Road. [E,6]	5.50
1.26	Cross intersection of Azalea Spring/Fern Flat Fire Road.	4.24
1.65	Deer Spring on left.	3.85
2.75	Cuyamaca Peak, designated turn-around point this trip. [F,4]	2.75
5.50	Back to start.	0.00

Trip No. 17C: Soapstone Loop, Cuyamaca Mountains

Length/Time: Eight miles; one hour loop

Season: Fall, spring; weekdays recommended

Difficulty: Three stars

Trail Surface: Fire road, 100%

Trail Grade: Climb: 900 feet; average grade, 4.3%

General:

A gentle, colorful slope through Upper Green Valley is a feature of this tour. A meadow runs along Soapstone Grade. Stretches with moon-like powder, dust and sand, along with occasional rocks, occur along Stonewall Fire Trail. A detour to Horse Camp (C, 7) will bring you within a stone's throw of Cuyamaca Lake.

Logistics

The trip begins at Park Headquarters, (H, 7). Parking is limited to two hours in the parking lot. The lot can be full on weekends. Roadside parking along Highway 79 is close by.

Miles from Start	Route Directions: 17C - Soapstone Loop, Cuyamaca Mountains	Miles to End
0.00	Head east from the parking lot staying to the right (south) side of the buildings. The trail heads northeast. [H,7]	7.90
0.50	Pass through gate.	7.40
0.86	Pass Cold Stream Trail on the left.	7.04
1.28	Pass Harvey Moore Trail on the right.	6.62

Miles from Start	Route Directions: 17C - Soapstone Loop, Cuyamaca Mountains	Miles to End
1.31	Turn left on Stonewall Creek Fire Road. (A sign at the entrance reads: "Cold Stream Trail 1/2 mile, Los Caballos 3 3/4 left, etc.") [G,8]	6.59
1.50	Start steep and rocky uphill for 1/2 mile.	6.40
2.23	Pass Cold Stream Trail on the left. [F,7]	5.67
3.51	Pass Los Vaqueros Trail on the left. [E,7]	4.39
3.59	Turn right on Soapstone Grade heading east. [D,8]	4.31
5.10	Turn right on Upper Green Valley Fire Road. [D,9]	2.80
5.45	Pass trail on the left. [E,9]	2.45
6.70	Pass Stonewall Grade Fire Road on the right. [G,8]	1.20
7.50	Back to gate.	0.40
7.90	Back to start.	0.00

Trip No. 17D: Green Valley, Cuyamaca Mountains

Length/Time: Seven miles, one hour loop

Season: Fall, spring; weekdays recommended

Difficulty: Three stars

Trail Surface: Dirt fire road, 95%; pavement (thru campground), 5%

Trail Grade: Climb: 900 feet; Average grade, 4.9%

General:

A trip on a typical mountain fire road heads uphill, for the most part, to an apex, then shoots down upon return. This trip provides the biker with a real workout. It bounces between 3800 feet - 4300 feet, four times: (1) down 400 feet to the Sweetwater River crossing; (2) up 500 feet through camp, to a peak on western chaparral slopes; (3) down 500 feet to the river again; and (4) back up 400 feet to the starting point. Long-distance views open up to the west, on the California Riding & Hiking Trail.

Logistics:

The trip begins at the Highway 79 roadside lot, [J, 6], just north of the posted "3.5 Miles" sign.

Miles from Start	Route Directions: 17D - Green Valley, Cuyamaca Mountains	Miles to End
0.00	Head west on South Boundary Fire Road from Highway 79. [J,6]	7.17
1.34	Pass trail on the left.	5.83
1.64	Stream crossing. Sweetwater River [J,5] Veer north.	5.53
1.84	Left (west) on South Boundary Fire Road. Sign: "To CA Riding and Hiking Trail." [I,5] (Right goes to Green Valley)	5.33
2.24	CA Riding and Hiking Trail comes in on the left (south), curve right, northerly.	4.93
2.64	Pass King Creek Fire Road on the left (west).	4.53
3.34	Pass Pine Ridge Trail on the right (southeast).	3.83
3.44	Turn right on Arroyo Seco Road. [H,5] Arroyo Seco Camp is 0.9 miles north of this junction. (Extra mileage not included.).	3.73
4.41	Turn right on paved road of Green Valley Campground. [I,5.5] Head to the southern most point of the campground which is a day-use parking lot.	2.76
4.78	Trail starts on the south end of the parking lot. [I,6] Head west down to the Sweetwater River.	2.39
5.53	Stay left onto South Boundary Fire Road. [J,5] South, then east, retracing the initial route.	1.64
7.17	Back to start at West Boundary Fire Road/East Mesa Road.	0.00

Trip No. 17E: Merigan Fire Road

Length/Time: Six miles; one hour round trip

Season: Fall, spring; weekdays recommended

Difficulty: Three stars

Trail Surface: Fire road, 50%; Highway 79, 50%

Trail Grade: Climb: 800 feet; average grade, 5.3%

General:
    As the trip with the lowest elevations in the Cuyamacas, this trip is warmer and drier. It includes two short, steep climbs with some rocks. The trail has a sandy start, a refreshing amount of woodland shade, and a satisfying amount of up-down variation. The return on pavement is a gradual descent, about 15 minutes long. The minimal shoulder on Highway 79 becomes a tense

ten minute stretch, during afternoon weekend traffic.

Logistics:

The trip is located in the southernmost area of Cuyamaca Park. It begins at the parking lot, (N, 4), on the north side of Viejas Boulevard in Descanso, just east of the town's main intersection.

Miles from Start	Route Directions: 17E - Cuyamaca: Merigan Fire Road	Miles to End
0.0	Head north and uphill on Merigan Fire Road, from Viejas Boulevard, paralleling Sweetwater River. [N,4]	5.7
2.1	Pass Sweetwater Trail on the left. Curve right (southeast).	3.6
3.2	Turn right heading downhill and south on Highway 79.[L,6]	2.5
4.8	Turn right, heading west on Viejas Boulevard into Descanso. [N,6]	0.9
5.7	Back to start.	0.0

MERIGAN FIRE ROAD enters the southern tip of Cuyamaca State Park from Descanso and offers abundant shade and wading pools along the Sweetwater River. - LL

CUYAMACA PEAK (elev. 6,512 ft.) punctuates the skyline north of the Sweetwater River near Descanso, portal to San Diego's finest, close-in mountain biking area. - LL

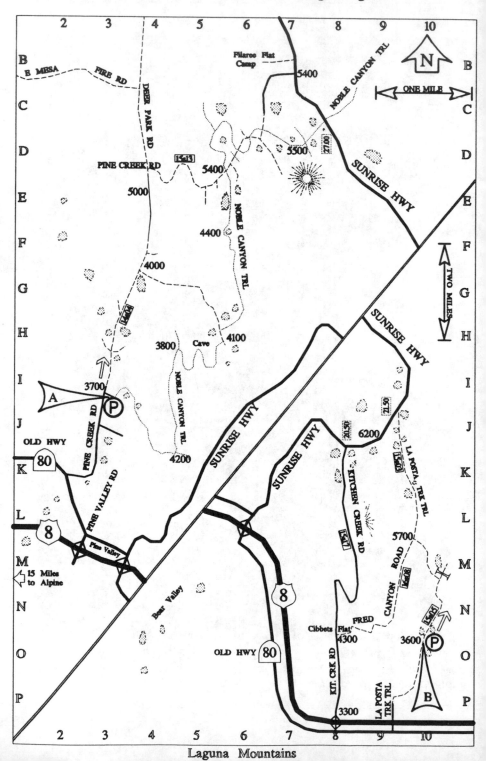

Laguna Mountains

Tour No.:   18

Title: Laguna Mountains

Overview:
"Little sister" to the Cuyamacas, the Laguna Range is a slightly warmer and drier sample of this favorite mountainous region. That works well for bikers, as it causes the "perfect weather band" to shift east to the Lagunas, when the Cuyamacas are becoming nippy, late in autumn. This progression reverses direction in spring, naturally, when the Lagunas become too hot. All of this prolongs the season for biking - in basically the same mountains! Be sure to get Harrison's <u>Recreation Map of the San Diego Back Country</u>, available in most bookstores in the county.

Trip No. 18A: Noble Canyon

Length/Time: 18 miles; three hours round trip

Season: Fall, spring; weekdays recommended

Difficulty: Five stars

Trail Surface: Fire road, 40%; difficult single track, 40%; paved, 20%

Trail Grade: Climb: 2600 feet; average grade, 5.5%

General:
The feeling of being immersed in nature is most intense on a single-file path, as it allows plants and shade to make an almost complete circle around you. The Noble Canyon Scenic Trail, as the return half of Trip 18A, does this dramatically. You coast first through pines with that scent unique to light, high elevation air. Then the path drops through oak shaded canyons, occasionally swinging out over rocky ledges with vistas far below. Although this is a very beautiful area, it takes nimble technical skills to enjoy and becomes demanding at times. The danger develops where this single-lane path is etched high upon a steep mountain face. Acknowledging a horse's right-of-way by "stepping off to the downside of the trail," may translate to, "tie a rope to the nearest rock and hang on!" Pedaling back to the nearest suitable spot can be aggravating, but as is usual, such gracious behavior is commonly required on a weekend.

Logistics:
This trip is located between Pine Valley and Laguna Mountain. The area is about a 1-1/2 hour drive from the ocean on Interstate 8. Exit I-8 at Pine Valley Road and proceed north. Turn left onto Highway 80, continue one mile and turn right onto Pine Creek Road. Proceed up another mile and park in the vicinity of the Noble Canyon Trail sign, [I, 3].

Miles from Start	Route Directions: 18A - Laguna Mountain: Noble Canyon	Miles to End
0.00	Head north on Pine Creek Road from the Noble Canyon Trailhead parking lot. [I,3]	18.00
0.10	Pavement ends.	17.90
0.49	Four-way intersection, take middle road.	17.51
1.07	Stay to the right. Deer Park Road, USFS 14s04.	16.93
2.04	Pass trail on the right.	15.96
2.43	Pass trail on the right.	15.57
2.62	Pavement starts. [F,4]	15.38
3.30	Pavement ends, cross cattle guard and turn right on road signed Pine Creek Road, {Forest Service #15s13}, heading east and uphill. [D,4]	14.70
4.20	Pass trail on the right. [E,5] (Stay on the main gravel road the next couple miles, there will be many roads intersecting in this area.)	13.80
6.14	Sign: "Laguna Mountain Recreation Area."	11.86
6.16	Turn left. [D,6.5]	11.84
6.53	Pavement starts up again, ecological study area on left.	11.47
7.27	Turn right on Sunrise Highway, heading southeast. [B,7]	10.73
7.72	Pass mile marker "27.5"	10.28
7.85	Turn right heading west on signed Noble Canyon Trail, (single track). [C,8]	10.15
7.95	Pass Big Laguna Trail, on the left. Continue west.	10.05
8.53	High point (5,500 ft.) for the trip.	9.47
8.94	Cross {15s13}.	9.06
8.98	Cross {15s13}, and a cattle guard diagonally. [D,6]	9.02
9.12	Cross (15s13}.	8.88
10.01	Pass Indian Creek Trail on the right.	7.99
10.72	Cross {15s13} for the last time! Work southwesterly.	7.28
11.17	Pass through gate. (Keep closed). [E,6] Descend Noble Canyon.	6.83
13.93	Pass cave on the right. [H,5]	4.07
15.14	Pass trail on the right. (Some uphill coming soon)	2.86
17.16	Pass trail on the left. [K,5]	0.84
17.86	End of Noble Canyon Trail. [I,3]	0.14
18.00	Back to start.	0.00

Trip No. 18B: Thing Valley, Kitchen Creek

Length/Time: 27 miles; two hours round trip

Season: Fall, spring; weekdays recommended

Difficulty: Four stars

Trail Surface: Dirt road, 50%; paved road (light traffic), 40%; highway, 10%

Trail Grade: Climb: 3100 feet; average grade, 4.4%

General:

The low elevations in this area are covered mainly by chaparral, with trees appearing only above 5700 feet. The grind up La Posta Truck Trail is a long one, and the trail gets eroded after the left turn at [M,10]. After the intersection with Fred Canyon Road, La Posta Truck Trail is maintained again, to some degree. The downhill on Kitchen Creek Road is one of the best in the area. It is paved, steep, and sees little traffic. A detour on Fred Canyon will shorten the trip both in distance and elevation, an option for the weary.

Logistics:

The trip area is located 10 miles southeast of Pine Valley. Exit I-8 near Cameron Forest Station at Kitchen Creek Road and proceed south, (P, 8). Turn left (east) on old Highway 80 and proceed 2.9 miles to La Posta Truck Trail. Turn left (north), pass under I-8 and after about 2 miles park at the first wooded area (O, 10).

KITCHEN CREEK is part of a major watershed in south central San Diego County that drains the Lagunas south into Baja rather than east to the desert or west into the Sweetwater system. - SB

Miles from Start	Route Directions: 18B - Thing Valley, Kitchen Creek	Miles to End
0.00	Head north on the mild uphill of La Posta Truck Trail, (labeled Thing Valley Road on Cleveland National Forest Map, and AAA map {15s05}). [O,10]	26.58
1.26	Pass a trail on the left and cross a gate that, at times, may be closed to keep motorized traffic out. [N,10]	25.32
3.78	Turn left onto Morris Randy Road. (Trail on right dead-ends into a gate and private property in Thing Valley.). [M,10] Trail gets steeper and rougher starting here.	22.80
5.72	Reach the three-way intersection of La Posta Truck Trail and Fred Canyon Road. Turn right and head north on La Posta Truck Trail, soon coming into pine trees. [L/M,10] (Option: At this point you could shorten the trip seven miles by taking a left on Fred Canyon Road heading southwest. You will miss all the pines and the best downhill though! This seven mile short-cut not subtracted from trip mileage).	20.86
6.50	Pass through gate, 15s03. [L,10]	20.08
7.95	Pass Pacific Crest Trail on the left.	18.63
8.54	Stay left at sign: "Laguna Mountain Recreation Area." [J,9]	18.04
9.02	Turn left and head west on Sunrise Highway, (north end of La Posta Road). Gate sometimes locked here, to keep motorized traffic out. [J,9]	17.56
11.06	Turn left on Kitchen Creek Road, and brace yourself for the downhill of your life! Use caution, there is gravel in some of the turns, 15s17. [J,8]	15.52
16.88	Kitchen Creek Road widens, center stripe starts.	9.70
17.56	Pass Cibbets Flat campground on the left. This is the southwest end of Fred Canyon Road.	9.02
20.18	Pass through a mile of shooting area. [O,8] Cross I-8.	6.40
21.83	Turn left heading east on Old Highway 80. [Q,8]	4.75
24.54	Turn left heading north on La Posta Truck Trail. [Q,9]	2.04
26.58	Back to start.	0.00

LAGUNA MOUNTAIN RIDING TRAILS are shared by a variety of recreationists. Right-of-way goes to those on two legs or four. - LL

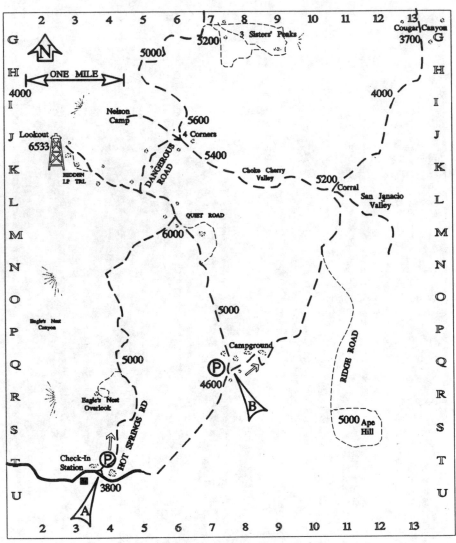

Los Coyotes Indian Reservation

Tour No.:   19

Title: Los Coyotes Indian Reservation

Overview:
   The highest point in our county is on the Los Coyotes Indian Reservation at Hot Springs Lookout, 6533 feet above sea level [J, 2]. This area is open year-round, but special arrangements are necessary if you plan to be there other than on a weekend. The front gate is attended from 8:00 a.m. to 5:00 p.m. on Fridays through Sundays and there is a small fee for day use ($1). Call 782-3269 after 6 p.m. for further information, or write to Banning Taylor, POB 249, Warner Springs, CA 92086. The reservation has a good growth of trees, especially at the higher elevations. Although the area is in the same elevation range as the Cuyamacas, it seems somewhat drier and warmer. An outstanding feature of this place is the lack of people. A whole network of beautiful trails can be enjoyed without the hassle of overpopulation - especially on the weekends! Most of the trails are labeled, which makes it fairly easy to find your way around. And maybe the best thing about this area, to many mountain bikers, is that the trails here are probably the smoothest in the county. It is almost impossible to find a rock on a trail throughout the entire area! Use also the Sidekick Map, Los Coyotes I. R. available at major bookstores.

Trip No. 19A: Los Coyotes Indian Reservation, Hot Springs Mountain

Length/Time: 14 miles; two hours round trip

Season: Fall, spring

Difficulty: Three stars

Trail Surface: Graded dirt road, 100%

Trail Grade: Climb: 2900 feet; average grade, 7.6%

General:
   This trip features a run to the lookout tower on a nice dirt road and return via any of several routes. This trip will put the "mountain" back in "mountain bike!" Serious gains in altitude occur. Most are on a steady grade, so setting a comfortable pace from the start is a must for the almost 3000 feet of climb encountered. Beautiful forests begin about halfway up Hot Springs Road. On a bright day, the shade is appreciated. The view from the abandoned tower at the summit is breathtaking. On certain days, a company out of Warner Springs takes gliders over Hot Springs Mountain. They are fun to watch as they make their spiraling descent.

Logistics:

Take Highway 79 to Warner Springs and at Mile Marker 35, turn east on Camino San Ignacio. Stay to the right on Los Tules Road and continue 4-1/2 miles to the entrance station of the reservation. The intersection of Hot Springs Mountain Road is 1/10 mile past the entrance station. Park in that area, [T,4].

Miles to End	Route Directions: 19A - Los Coyotes Indian Reservation: Hot Springs Mountain	Miles from Start
0.00	Head north and uphill on Hot Springs Road, stay on the main wide trail. [T,4]	14.36
5.00	Pass major road on the right. [L,6] (It leads to the campground at [Q,8].)	9.36
5.53	Pass Dangerous Road on the right.	8.83
7.18	Arrive at lookout tower. Check it out and head back the same way you came up. This is the designated turn-around point for this trip. [J,3]	7.18
9.36	Stay to the right, taking the same trail you came up on. (Option: For variety, here you could turn left at [L,6] and take the steeper descent back through the campground via Cross Over Road. It is only 1/3 mile longer, back to start.)	5.00
14.36	Back to start. [T,4]	0.00

BACKPACKERS, too, enjoy the tranquility and distant vistas of Los Coyotes. - LL

Trip No. 19B: North Border, Los Coyotes Indian Reservation

Length/Time:	16 miles, two hours, two-way trip
Season:	Fall, spring
Difficulty:	Three stars
Trail Surface:	Graded dirt road, 80%; eroded dirt road, 20%
Trail Grade:	Climb: 1800 feet; average grade, 4.4%

General:
This trip is milder through the reservation than was Trip 19A. Views of Anza-Borrego Desert to the east may be seen. The route passes meadows and corrals with horses and cows. There are also some neat boulders in the northern section of the reservation.

Logistics:
To get to the reservation, follow directions described in Trip 19A. From the entrance station, drive on the main road to the campground [Q,8] and park in the parking area.

Miles from Start	Route Directions: 19B - Los Coyotes Indian Reservation: North Border	Miles to End
0.00	From the campground, head east on main wide trail. [Q,8]	15.52
1.57	Stay to the left.	13.95
2.91	Pass corral on the right in San Ignacio. Turn left, heading west. [L,11]	12.61
5.24	Arrive at 4-Corners. [J,6] Turn right heading north.	10.28
5.29	Pass Ladybug Lane on the left (This rejoins below.)	10.23
5.82	Pass Creek Road on the right (AKA Hot Dog Hill).	9.70
7.08	Pass Up-Down Hill on the left (leads to Ladybug Lane).	8.44
7.47	Arrive at 4-way intersection. Go straight. [G,7]	8.05
7.76	Low-Bridge Loop is on the left. From here, you are on your own to explore, there are several trails heading out and they all get progressively more difficult. This is the designated turn-around point for this trip. Head back the same way you came in. (No mileage is added to trip total for exploring from this point.). Use the Sidekick Map for details here.	7.76
15.52	Back to start.	0.00

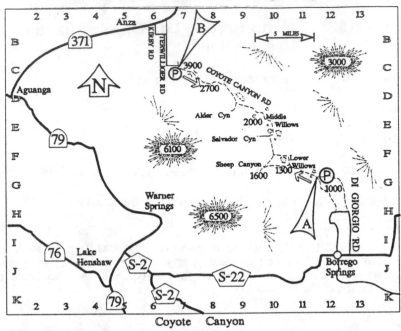

Coyote   Canyon

MOUNTAIN BIKING RULES IN ANZA-BORREGO DESERT STATE PARK

The California Motor Vehicle Code applies to paved and approved dirt routes of travel within the State Park (which is virtually all of the desert areas of San Diego County). The law requires that "all vehicles (including bicycles) must remain on established roads."

The following excerpt is from the current edition of the Anza-Borrego Desert State Park newspaper, published by the Anza-Borrego Desert Natural History Association.

WHERE MAY WE RIDE OUR MOUNTAIN BIKES?
by Bob Theriault, State Park Ranger

The answer to this often-asked question is: On any paved roadway or Jeep road. There are more than 500 miles of such roads traversing the park.

Coyote Canyon and Grapevine Canyon are suitable and frequently used by mountain bikers. Coyote Canyon is closed from June 15 to September 16. The Blair Valley area is relatively flat and scenic as well. Oriflamme Canyon is very steep and physically demanding as it climbs high above the desert floor into the chaparral.

Pedaling in deep sand is no fun. Avoid sandy areas.

Remember, bicycles are not allowed on any foot paths, including nature trails and the Pacific Crest Trail. Riders must stay on the roadways at all times and may not venture off searching for "firmer ground."

For a safe visit carefully plan your ride and do not overextend yourself. Enjoy exploring Anza-Borrego.

Tour No.: 20

Title: Coyote Canyon

Overview:

This is the site of the annual Coyote Canyon Clunker Classic mountain bike ride, each winter. Coyote Canyon is closed each year from June 16th to September 16th to protect the watering needs of bighorn sheep in the area. Every September 17th people rush in to see if they can spot bighorns that might have become used to having the area all to themselves! Summer is not the time to be out here, so the closure is appropriate. Springs maintain a flow of water in Coyote Creek year-round, and in Trip 20A the trail actually becomes the stream for about a mile in what is called Middle Willows. Rugged Coyote Canyon is a popular area in Anza-Borrego Desert State Park, and may be humming with hikers, bikers, and four-wheelers, on winter weekends. Use also the Sidekick Coyote Canyon Map available at major bookstores.

Trip No. 20A: Sheep Canyon, Collins Valley Loop

Length/Time: 12 miles, two hours round trip

Season: Fall through spring

Difficulty: Four stars

Trail Surface: Sand washes, 75%; dirt road, 25%

Trail Grade: Climb: 800 feet; average grade, 2.5%

General:

This trip up is a counterclockwise loop of Collins Valley, with a spur option to Sheep Canyon Camp. It contains some deep sand, so wide tires will be a plus. At [F,10], where the trip is designed to start a loop back south and return, it is possible to continue north as far as Anza in Riverside County (see Trip 20B below). It might be enough to continue to Middle Willows though, which is quite a sight with all its vegetation and flowing water.

Logistics:

Head north from the center of Borrego Springs, (Christmas Circle), on Borrego Springs Road. It curves around and heads east. Turn left, heading north on Di Giorgio Road. This turns to dirt and takes you into the park. On the right will be "Desert Gardens," and a small display. This is the best place to park, if you have anything other than a truck, because some deep dips are just past this point. You can follow the directions of Trip 20A from here to the first water-crossing if you want to park further north.

Miles from Start	Route Directions: 20A - Sheep Canyon, Collins Valley Loop	Miles to End
0.00	From Desert Gardens, [G,12], head west on the dirt road.	11.79
0.61	Streambed crossing, pass horse trail to Ocotillo Flat on the right. "First Crossing."	11.18
0.65	Turn right on wide trail heading north (left goes to Horse Camp).	11.14
1.60	Water crossing, stay to the right once across. "Second Crossing."	10.19
1.94	Pass through gate, (closure point June 16-Sept. 15)	9.85
2.18	Stay left and go through another water crossing. "Third Crossing."	9.61
2.38	Start of a steep rocky climb. Lower Willows By-pass.	9.41
2.96	End of steep climb!	8.83
3.25	Pass Santa Catarina Spring on the right, stay left following signs "to Anza."	8.54
3.98	Turn right on trail "to Anza." (Trail on left goes to Sheep Canyon.)	7.81
5.14	Turn left heading west towards Sheep Canyon. [F,10] Now follow signs "to Borrego."	6.65
6.31	Make a hard left turn heading southeast "to Borrego."	5.48
7.81	Turn right on trail heading south "to Borrego." Now you are on the same trail you came in on. Take it all the way back to start.	3.98
11.79	Back to start at Desert Gardens.	0.00

Trip No. 20B: Top to Bottom, Anza to Borrego

Length/Time: 19 miles; three hours, one-way trip

Season: Fall through spring (closed June 15 - September 15)

Difficulty: Five stars

Trail Surface: Wide dirt road, 40%; sandy wash, 30%; eroded, rocky, dirt road, 25%; under water, 5%

Trail Grade: Climb/descend: 200/3000 feet; average grade, 3.3%

General:
       This is the whole enchilada; you won't feel you have missed anything when done with this trip - it has substance! It has over a thousand feet of rocky

descent in the first three miles, a mile of riding in a river, stretches of deep sand, and several stream crossings! Luckily it is all downhill and one-way, but that means setting up a two-car shuttle of some sort. A two-way trip through this area would be pretty rough, considering the 3200 feet of elevation gain, but it is possible. Starting from the bottom, near Borrego Springs, would probably be best so that the downhill would be on the way back.

Logistics:

Setting up a two car shuttle for a one-way trip through Coyote Canyon is problematic because of the 75 miles of slow road between the starting point and the finish point. We recommend that you find someone who feels like taking a nice Sunday drive. She can drop you off at the top, and pick you up at the bottom. To get to the top, take Highway 371 from Aguanga. Just east of Anza, take Terwilliger Road south about four miles. Coyote Canyon Road will be a graded road on the left heading east, (the road sign is a short, white, wooden post). Follow that around, turning south, and eventually you will get to the Anza-Borrego Desert State Park sign and entry gate [C,7]. Drop off here. To get the car to the south end of Coyote Canyon, follow the map to Borrego Springs, (Highway 371 to 79 to S-2 to S-22), and then refer to the Logistics Section for Trip 20A to get to Desert Gardens [G,12], or plan to pedal all the way into Borrego Springs, (an extra eight miles). Christmas Circle [I/J, 12] is a good central location in the valley.

Miles from Start	Route Directions: 20B - Top to Bottom, Anza to Borrego	Miles to End
0.00	From the entrance gate to the Anza-Borrego State Park (closure point June 16-Sept. 15) head south on the trail, (Coyote Canyon road). [C,7]	18.43
0.50	Cross the Pacific Crest Trail (no wheels).	17.93
0.97	Start of steep descent along Nance Canyon.	17.46
2.76	End of steep descent, "Turkey Track," and stream.	15.67
5.67	Pass trail to Alder Canyon on the right. [D,9]	12.76
6.40	Pass stone shack, "Bailey Line Shack." Upper Willows.	12.03
7.28	"Anza Expedition" historical marker.	11.15
9.25	The trail is a flowing streambed at Middle Willows. [E,10]	9.18
10.00	End of underwater riding!	8.43
12.17	Stay left at the Salvador Canyon junction.	6.26
13.29	Stay left at the north Sheep Canyon junction. [F,10]	5.14
14.45	Stay left heading southeast, following signs "to Borrego." (Right goes to Sheep Canyon.)	3.98
15.18	Pass Santa Catarina Spring and ECV monument on the left.	3.25
15.47	Start of short rocky downhill, "Lower Willows By-pass."	2.96

Miles from Start	Route Directions: 20B - Top to Bottom, Anza to Borrego	Miles to End
16.25	Water crossing, then stay right on main trail heading south. "Third Crossing."	2.18
16.49	Pass through gate, (closure point June 16-Sept. 15).	1.94
16.83	Water crossing. "Second Crossing."	1.60
17.78	Turn left on trail heading east towards Di Giorgio Road. "First Crossing."	0.65
18.43	Desert Gardens on left, end of trail. (It is 8.7 miles to Christmas Circle in Borrego Springs from here.)	0.00

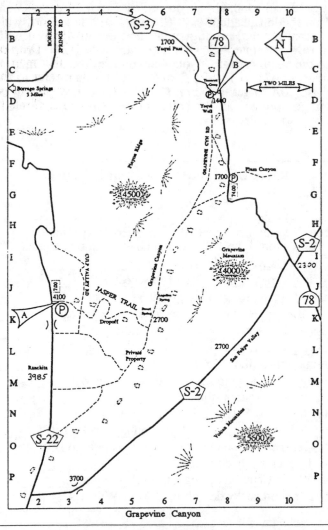

Grapevine Canyon

Tour No.:   21

Title: Grapevine Canyon

Overview:
Here is another area with a big downhill one-way, (Trip 21A, 3200 feet). Most will therefore prefer to be dropped off at the top and be picked up at the bottom. But for those with endurance, a round trip (3500 feet of climbing) is possible using a stretch of Highway 78 and county roads. The off-road trails here are usually smooth and occasionally sandy. The steepest sections occur on Jasper Trail, (note elevations on map between S-22 and Grapevine!). Grapevine Canyon Road is a powerline road and was developed on harder ground than Jasper Trail. Grapevine stays in fairly good repair. There is quite a variety of vegetation in this tour due to the change in elevation, and some nice long distance views open up on Jasper Trail. Grapevine Canyon has strips of riparian vegetation, and flowing springs provide water. Yaqui Well is an oasis and provides an opportunity to spy on birds and other desert creatures.

Trip No. 21A: Ranchita to Tamarisk Grove Campground via Jasper Trail (one-way)

Length/Time: 13 miles; two hours, one-way trip

Season: Fall through spring

Difficulty: Three stars

Trail Surface: Dirt road, 70%; sandy road, 30%

Trail Grade: Climb/Descend: 500/3000 feet, average grade, 5.0%

General:
The shortest trip is to ride only the steep downhill on Jasper Trail and bail out early by heading south to Plum Canyon, ending the trip there, [G,8].

Logistics:
The trip is in the vicinity of Ranchita, 10 miles west of Borrego Springs. In order to leave "number two" car at end-of-tour, take Highway 78 east out of Julian to either ending point, [G, 8] Plum Canyon or [C, 7] Tamarisk Grove. Return west with "number one" car on Highway 78 to Highway S-2 at Scissors Crossing and turn right. Proceed northwest through San Felipe Valley to Highway S-22 and turn right (east) again. After Mile Marker 6 you will cross the Anza-Borrego Desert State Park boundary line at the summit. Off to the right-hand side of road, prior to reaching Mile Marker 7, is the Jasper Trail. It is hard to spot so proceed slowly. Park "number one" car at Jasper Trailhead [J, 3].

Miles to End	Route Directions: 21A - Ranchita to Tamarisk Grove via Jasper Trail	Miles from Start
0.00	Head south on Jasper Trail from S-22. [J/K,3]	13.10
0.49	Pass trail on left.	12.61
1.36	Cross Culp Valley Road, continue south on Jasper Trail. [K,3]	11.74
2.23	Stay to the right. (Left dead-ends just overcrest.). [K,4]	10.87
3.11	Two drop-offs	9.99
5.04	Jasper Trail ends, left (east) on Grapevine Canyon. [K,6]	8.06
5.34	Stuart Spring on the left, (labeled).	7.76
6.50	Stay left. (Right is more scenic because it stays down by the stream bed and big trees, but it dead-ends). [J,6]	6.60
9.02	Turn left towards Yaqui Well, (becomes power line road.) [G,7]	4.08
(9.02)	(Turn right to optional trip end at Plum Canyon.).	(1.95)
10.96	Pass trail on right. (Leads towards Plum Canyon). [F,8]	2.14
12.61	Yaqui Well on left. Interesting detour! (200 ft. to the north, follow signs). [D,7]	0.49
13.10	End of trip, highway S-3.	0.00

Trip No. 21B: Yaqui Well to Jasper Trail (two-way, out and back to B)

Length/Time: 16 miles; three hours, two-way trip

Season: Fall through spring

Difficulty: Two stars

Trail Surface: Dirt road, 100%

Trail Grade: Climb: 1500 feet; average grade, 3.5%

General:
    This trip utilizes the easier section of this trip - Grapevine Canyon Road. It is a dirt road with no serious climbing involved. It has large trees next to it in several places which may inspire exploratory detours. Flowing springs are near the south end of Jasper Trail; Stuart Spring is signed and visible from the trail.

Logistics:
    This trip begins 10 miles south of Borrego Springs on County Road S-3, (Yaqui Pass Road), one block north of Highway 78. The trail begins with a sign, "To Yaqui Well." Park anywhere in that area, [D,7].

Miles from Start	Route Directions: 21B -Yaqui Well to Jasper Trail	Miles to End
0.00	Head west on Grapevine Canyon Road. (Labeled Yaqui Well Camp at Highway S-3). [D,7]	16.12
0.49	Yaqui Well on right. Interesting detour! (200 ft. to the north, follow signs).	15.63
2.14	Stay to the right on power line road. (Left leads towards Plum Canyon). [E,7]	13.98
4.08	Pass trail on left. (It leads towards Plum Canyon). [G,7]	12.04
6.60	Stay to the right. (Left leads to an interesting detour in the stream bed). [J,6]	9.52
7.76	Stuart Spring on the right, (labeled).	8.36
8.06	Intersect with Jasper Trail on the right. This is designated turn-around point for this trip, head back the same way you came. (Straight ahead on Grapevine Canyon Road heads into private property, and right on Jasper gets steep uphill.) [K,6]	8.06
12.04	(Option: on your way back, turn right here, [G,7], towards Plum Canyon (instead of left to Yaqui Well) and take a little bit of Grapevine Wash back, then jump onto highway 78 when you get tired of that, back to start. This extra 2 miles of detour not added into trip mileage).	4.08
16.12	Back to start.	0.00

Trip No. 21C: Tamarisk Grove, San Felipe, Jasper Trail - Round Trip

Length/Time: 38 miles; five hours, round trip

Season: Fall through spring

Difficulty: Four stars

Trail Surface: Public road, 65%; steep trail, 15%; wide dirt trail, 20%

Trail Grade: Climb: 3700 feet; average grade, 3.7%

General:

No wimps! 3700 feet of elevation gain will weed out the weaklings on this trip. It starts out with a deceptively mild grade on Highway 78, but before long, you'll be downshifting to compensate for the tilting landscape. There are short breaks from the climb in a few stretches, but it's not really over until

Jasper Trail is reached, and even then, you still have a 500 foot climb, and all in one stretch [K,4]. Some may prefer the reverse trip, counter-clockwise, so all the downhill is on pavement. The advantage is that you won't have to transfer the hard work of the climb to your brake pads on the downhill, as you will, to a large extent, on Jasper Trail. The main drawback is that you may be walking your bike up some of the grades, heading north on Jasper Trail. It's a trade-off!

Logistics:

This trip begins 10 miles south of Borrego Springs on County Road S-3, (Yaqui Pass Road), one block north of Highway 78 just west of Tamarisk Grove Campground. The trail begins with a sign, "To Yaqui Well." Park anywhere in that area, [D,7].

Miles from Start	Route Directions: 21C - Tamarisk Grove, San Felipe, Jasper Trail -Round Trip	Miles to End
0.0	Head south one block to Highway 78 from the east end of Grapevine Canyon Road. [D,7]	38.1
0.1	Turn right heading west on Highway 78.	38.0
6.5	"Scissors Crossing." Turn right heading northwest and uphill on County Road S-2, (San Felipe Road). [I,10]	31.6
19.0	Turn right heading east on County Road S-22, (Montezuma Valley Road). [Q,2]	19.1
25.0	Just before mile marker "7.0," turn right on Jasper Trail. It is sort of hidden so look carefully, it is signed. [J/K,3]	13.1
25.5	Pass trail on left.	12.6
26.4	Cross Culp Valley Road, continue south on Jasper Trail. [K,3]	11.7
27.2	Stay to the right. (Left dead-ends just over the crest.). [K,4]	10.9
28.1	Two small drop-offs.	10.0
30.0	Jasper Trail ends, left on Grapevine Canyon. [K,6]	8.1
30.3	Stuart Spring on the left, (labeled).	7.8
31.5	Stay left. (Right is more scenic because it stays down by the stream bed and big trees, but it dead-ends). [J,6]	6.6
34.0	Turn left towards Yaqui Well, (becomes power line road.) [G,7]	4.1
(34.0)	(Turn right to optional trip end at Plum Canyon). 4.1	(2.0)
36.0	Pass trail on right. (Leads towards Plum Canyon). [F,8]	2.1
37.6	Yaqui Well on left. Interesting detour! (200 ft. to the north, follow signs). [D,7]	0.5
38.1	End of trip, highway S-3.	0.00

GRAPEVINE CANYON is a fault controlled drainage revealed by such features as its linearity and multiple springs in-line including Stuart Spring (pictured above) just east of the Jasper Trail junction. - LL

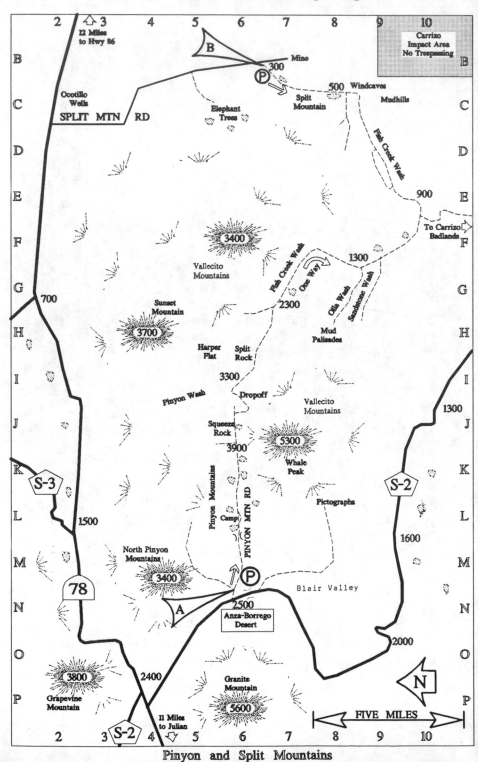

Pinyon and Split Mountains

Tour No.:   22

Title: Pinyon and Split Mountains

Overview:
    One-way travel is required on the dirt roads of this area, from Pinyon Mountain on the west to Split Mountain on the east. This is because a large portion of the route near its center (Squeeze Rock and the Drop-Off) are in canyons which are just wide enough for one vehicle. There are other reasons to go in the prescribed direction. For one, it is mostly downhill with about 3000 feet of altitude loss. Then there is the Drop-Off, [1, 6] - this one is scary in just walking your mountain bike down! There is a lot of sand in this area so wide tires are essential. The scenic diversity from one end of the tour to the other is impressive. The Pinyon end is high desert, with an elevation of around 4000 feet and an average rainfall of about 15 inches per year. The Split Mountain end is around sea level, and only gets around 3 inches of rain per year. The west side has some unique vegetation, including pinyon pine. The east end has fossil shell reefs and the Wind Caves, formations similar to those in the Borrego Badlands. Most of the east half trail is very sandy and occasionally becomes washboard.

Trip No. 22A:	**Pinyon to Split Mountain (one-way)**
Length/Time:	28 miles; four hours one-way
Season:	Fall through spring
Difficulty:	Four stars
Trail Surface:	Wide dirt road, 30%; sand/dirt wash, 70%
Trail Grade:	Climb/descend: 1300/3000 feet; average grade, 2.9%

General:
    This trip is a long one. A trip through the whole area will require a shuttle using two cars, one parked at end-of-tour and the other at start-of-tour. All of these arrangements, however, will more than pay off because this trip is a blast! It's one with a lot of coasting through a variety of scenery. There is some climbing and there are occasional sections of heavy sand and rocks. Beware of the Drop-off. It's nutty trying to descend on anything but your feet. Bring plenty of water and some food.

Logistics:

To get to end-of-trip and the drop-off of one vehicle, take Highway 78 east out of Julian, proceed about 30 miles to Ocotillo Wells and turn right, heading south on Split Mountain Road [C, 2]. About eight miles down on the right will be the turn-off to Fish Creek Wash. Leave the "number one" car here, then retrace your route back to Highway 78, heading west in the "number two" car. Turn left (southeast) on County Road S-2 at Scissors Crossing. Just past (southeast of) Mile Marker 21 is the turn-off to the "Pinyon Mountain Area," on the left, just after you cross the Anza-Borrego Desert State Park boundary.

Miles from Start	Route Directions: 22A - Pinyon Mountain to Split Mountain	Miles to End
0.00	Head east on the right fork of the mildly sandy Pinyon Mountain Road from S-2. [N,6] Commence steep climb.	28.03
3.69	Pass through camping area. Stay on the main traveled trail heading east. All other trails will either dead-end into campsites or weave their way back to the main trail. [L,6]	24.34
5.24	High point of the trip (3,900 ft.).	22.79
5.34	Pass a trail on the left. [K,6]	22.69
6.50	Go through "the squeeze", (A slot of solid rock about 7 ft. wide that many four-wheeled vehicles have trouble with)!	21.53
6.98	Turn right on a rocky trail heading uphill. (Straight ahead on the wash leads down to a sheer drop-off in a few hundred feet. It is an interesting detour to see.) [J,6]	21.05
7.37	Pinyon Mountain Dropoff, AKA Heart Attack Hill. Carefully walk your bike down this challenge.	20.66
8.25	Stay right on the traveled trail at Harper Flat. Go uphill for roughly a mile to Hapaha Flat. [I,6]	19.78
11.74	Pass McCain Spring Hiking Trail on left. [G,7]	16.29
16.01	Pass Olla Wash on right.	12.02
16.68	Pass Sandstone Wash on right	11.35
19.21	Pass Diablo Drop-off Wash on right. [E/F,10]	8.82
23.86	Fossil reef and wind caves on right. Interesting detour!	4.17
24.15	Pass Fish Creek North Fork on left. [C,8] Enter Split Mountain.	3.88
26.68	Exit Split Mountain. Pass Fish Creek Primitive Camp on right	1.35
27.65	View of U. S. Gypsum Mine on right.	0.38
28.03	Split Mountain Road, end of trip. [B,6]	0.00

Trip No. 22B: Pinyon Mountain (two-way, out and back)

Length/Time: 11 miles, two hours, two-way trip

Season: Fall through spring

Difficulty: Three stars

Trail Surface: Wide dirt road, 30%; sand/dirt wash, 70%

Trail Grade: Climb: 1700 feet; average grade, 6.1%

General:

This tour is basically a short, two-way trip through the west end of the tour area. It includes views of Pinyon Pine and a ride around Pinyon Mountain Valley - a popular place to camp.

Logistics:

The trip area is about 12 miles east of Julian. Take Highway 78 east from Julian. Proceed about 10 miles and turn right at Scissors Crossing, onto S-2, proceeding south. After (driving) about 5 miles along S-2, you will see the Anza-Borrego Desert State Park sign. Almost immediately across the road is the sign which marks the entrance to the Pinyon Mountain Area. Park near the entrance area, [N, 6].

Miles from Start	Route Directions: 22B - Pinyon Mountain	Miles to End
0.00	Head east on the right fork of the mildly sandy Pinyon Mountain Road from S-2. [N,6]	10.48
3.69	Pass through camping area. Stay on the main traveled trail heading east. All other trails will either dead-end into campsites or weave their way back to the main trail. [L,6]	6.79
5.24	High point of trail (3,900 ft.) and the designated turn-around point. [K,6] (Option: Some awesome downhill is between here, and "the squeeze," to the east. Turn around at the squeeze and come back the same way. This 2.5 mile detour is not added into trip mileage).	5.24
6.79	Pass back through camping area. [L,6]	3.69
10.48	Back to start at Highway S-2 near Stage Trail store.	0.00

Trip No. 22C:　Fish Creek Wash and Split Mountian (two-way in and out)

Length/Time:	9 miles; two hours, two-way
Season:	Fall through spring, cool weather only
Difficulty:	Three stars
Trail Surface:	Dirt/sand wash, 100%
Trail Grade:	Climb: 200 feet; average grade, 0.2%

General:

This is a two-way trip through the east end of the trip area. There are geological formations in this area that appear to be from another world. The area south of Split Mountain was under an ocean millions of years ago and still shows it. The Elephant Knees, the folded rock anticline, mudhills, and sandstone cliffs are some of the wonders you will see. The Wind Caves are not accessible by mountain bike, but they are worth the hike. These spectacular formations are separated by miles of sandy wash, though, and a hot day precludes entry.

Logistics:

Drive south on Split Mountain Road from Ocotillo Wells [C, 2] eight miles to the Fish Creek Wash crossing, [B, 6]. Park in that area.

Miles from Start	Route Directions:　22C - Fish Creek Wash	Miles to End
0.00	Head west on the wide Fish Creek Wash from Split Mountain Road. [B,6]	9.40
1.35	Pass Fish Creek Camp on left. [B,7] Pass through Split Mountain, observing spectacular anticline at mile 3.5	8.05
3.88	Pass Fish Creek North Fork on right. [C,8]	5.52
4.17	Fossil reef and wind caves on left. Interesting hike!	5.23
4.70	Mudhills Wash and Elephant Knees interpretive panel. Turn around here.	4.70
9.40	Back to start.	0.00

SPLIT MOUNTAIN, formed by torrential flooding of normally dry Fish Creek, is known as "The Storybook of Time" for the chapters of earth history revealed here. - CDP

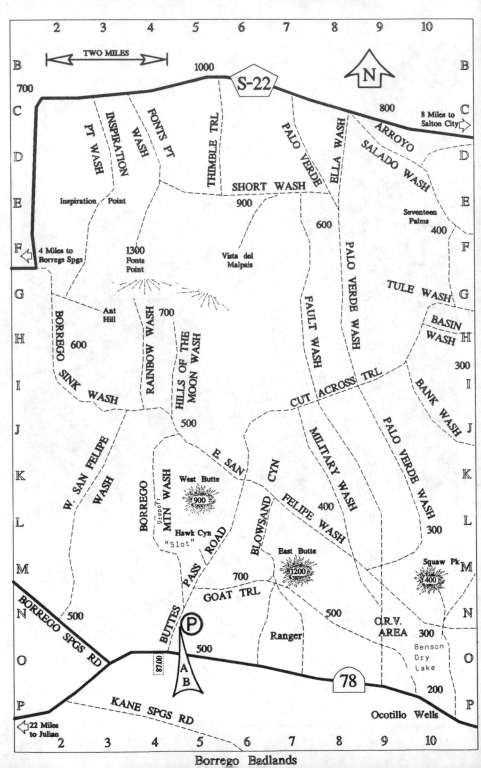

Borrego Badlands

Tour No.:   23

Title: Borrego Mountain and Badlands

Overview:

For atmospheric reasons, the desert frequently has most spectacular sunsets. Often there are shades of purple and orange in the late afternoon sky that never develop with such intensity along the coast. What a perfect cover for such an eerie looking place as the "badlands!" The soft mud/sand landscape is continually changing as the elements attack the serpentine razorback ridges. Wind and flash floods melt mountain sediments into and down the washes at a rapid rate. Not much can grow in such shifting soil, but the contours and contrasts of this mysterious terrain are weirdly interesting, even without vegetation! Fortunately, most of the trails here are labeled with signs, making it easy to chart locations and directions. In this area, as in all of Anza-Borrego Desert State Park, all vehicles including mountain bikes, must stay on the existing trails. The only exception is the Off-Road Vehicle (ORV) area which is centered around (N, 9). Most motorcycle activity is in the ORV area.

Most of the trails in this area are in the washes. This means sand, and sand usually isn't a lot of fun on a bike. Both trips described below were designed to cover the many diverse features of this area, using the "deep sand washes" as optional routes, rather than the main ones. The average high temperature from November to February is only about 5 degrees above that of San Diego. However, in summer Borrego Springs can be 30 degrees hotter. During May through September the tour area becomes the "real-bad lands!" Temperatures can soar to 120 degrees in July. Fall starts the rainy season with the usually mild rains reaching their peak frequency around January, then tapering off to almost nothing by the start of spring. In March and April the desert shows its true colors. Ocotillo, desert shrubs and cacti bristle with flowers and wildflowers generally come to life for a few days, after which austerity returns.

Trip No. 23A: Goat/Blowsand/San Felipe Wash (and Buttes Pass Alternate) Loop

Length/Time: 14 miles; three hours round trip, counterclockwise

Season: Fall through spring, cool weather only

Difficulty: Four stars

Trail Surface: Dirt road, 20%; washes, 70%; road, 10%

Trail Grade: Climb: 1100 feet; average grade, 2.9%

General:

Goat Trail, true to its name, winds through a challenging series of climbs to the highest point of this trip. Blowsand Canyon is one of those rare places where you might find sand fun - on a steep downhill! It's interesting, something like snow. Hills of the Moon and Rainbow Washes contain the type of scenery that the Badlands is famous for. Optional detours up these provide some tough pedaling, but the scenery is remarkable.

Logistics:

The Badlands area is west and north of Ocotillo Wells. The tour begins 22 miles east of Julian on Highway 78. It begins on the north side of the road, just east of Mile Marker 87.0, [O, 4].

Miles from Start	Route Directions: 23A - Goat Trail, Blowsand Canyon, and San Felipe Wash Loop	Miles to End
0.00	Head northeast on Buttes Pass Road from Highway 78. [O,4]	14.16
0.87	Turn right to stay on Buttes Pass Road. [N,5]	13.29
1.36	Turn right on Goat Trail heading uphill and east. [M,5]	12.80
2.91	Turn left heading east, then left heading north and downhill through Blowsand Canyon, (a large U-shaped turn). [M,7]	11.25
4.66	Turn left heading northwest in E. San Felipe Wash. [K,7]	9.50
5.43	Cross intersection of Buttes Pass Road/Cut Across Trail with San Felipe Wash. [K,6] Optional turnoff left (south) here, onto harder pack dirt up Buttes Pass and shortcut to Mile 1.36. Explore spectacular Hawk Canyon en route.	8.73
7.08	Pass Borrego Mountain Wash on left. [J,5]*	7.08
7.28	Hills of the Moon Wash on right. [J,5]	6.88
7.57	Rainbow Wash on right. [I,4].	6.59
7.86	Turn left in W. San Felipe Wash heading south. [J,3]	6.30
12.03	Turn left on paved Borrego Springs Road. [N,2]	2.13
12.71	Turn left on Highway 78. [O,3]	1.45
14.16	Back to start.	0.00

* Another optional shortcut left (south) up Borrego Mountain Wash, pushing bike up the Borrego Mountain dropoff to Desert Lookout above "The Slot" and on to the Highway 78 starting point. Sand travel is negligible beyond the drop-off. (See Trip 23B for details.).

Trip No. 23B: Drop-Off/Cut-Across/Palo Verde/ OWSVRA Loop

Length/Time: 28 miles; four hours round trip; clockwise

Season: Fall through spring, cool weather only

Difficulty: Three stars

Trail Surface: Dirt trail, 35%; wash, 50%; Highway 78, 15%

Trail Grade: Climb: 800 feet; average grade, 1.0%

General:

This is the "easier" of the two trips through the area It stays on a more level and firmer ground surface. The tour is planned so that the softer sand is on the downhills, harder pack on the ups. Example: up Palo Verde Wash, down Fault Wash is easier than visa-versa. As a central leg of this trip, the Cut-Across Trail is used because it is one of the only man-made trails here and is on solid ground. If you burn out, you can almost "fly" back on the hard packed Cut-Across Trail, taking it at any of the wash intersections.

Logistics:

The Badlands area is west and north of Ocotillo Wells and about 5 miles east of Borrego Springs. The tour begins 22 miles east of Julian on Highway 78. It begins on the north side of the road, just east of Mile Marker 87.0, [O, 4]. Park anywhere in that area.

Miles from Start	Route Directions: 23B - Drop-Off/Cut-Across/ Palo Verde/OWSVRA Loop	Miles to End
0.00	Head northeast on Buttes Pass Road from Highway 78. [O,4]	28.23
0.97	Turn left onto Borrego Mountain Wash and Desert Lookout. [N,5]	27.26
1.75	Take left trail, (right is a dead-end). [M,4] Above The Slot.	26.48
2.62	Steep downhill at Borrego Mountain Dropoff.	25.61
2.81	Turn left at bottom, (right is a dead-end into The Slot. [L,4]	25.42
2.91	Trail gets sandy with a hard drop over sandstone ledges.	25.32
3.78	Take left trail heading north. [K,4]	24.45
4.95	Turn right (east) in San Felipe Wash. [J,5]	23.28
6.69	Turn left (north) on Cut-Across Trail, which is a wash for 7/10 mile before it climbs out of the sand to the right (northeast). [K,6]	21.54

Miles from Start	Route Directions: 23B - Drop-Off/Cut-Across/ Palo Verde/OWSVRA Loop	Miles to End
8.92	Pass Military Wash on the right. [J,7] Optional shortcut to Ocotillo Wells by turning right (southeast) on any of these washes.	19.31
9.60	Cross Fault Wash.	18.63
10.09	Turn left heading north on Palo Verde Wash. [I,9]	18.14
13.39	Stay left on Palo Verde Wash, (Ella Wash is to the right). [E,8]	14.84
13.48	Turn left in Short Wash heading west. [E,8]	14.75
14.07	Turn left in Fault Wash heading south, then east for a bit, then stay south heading downhill. [E,7]	14.16
18.24	Cross Cut-Across Trail, still heading southeast in Fault Wash. [I,8] Enter OWSVRA and watch out!	9.99
20.56	Fault Wash turns into a road heading due south.	7.67
21.24	Cross San Felipe Wash. [M,9]	6.99
22.41	Cross Benson Lake Loop. [N,9]	5.82
23.34	Fault Wash ends at Highway 78, turn right. [P,9]	4.89
28.23	Back to start	0.00

BORREGO BADLANDS VISTA looking south across San Felipe Wash to Borrego Mountain Wash in the middle ground and Vallecito Mountains on the horizon. - CDP

"THE SLOT" is the head of Borrego Mountain Wash, about two miles northwest of the Buttes Pass/Hwy. 78 junction which begins Trips 23A and 23B

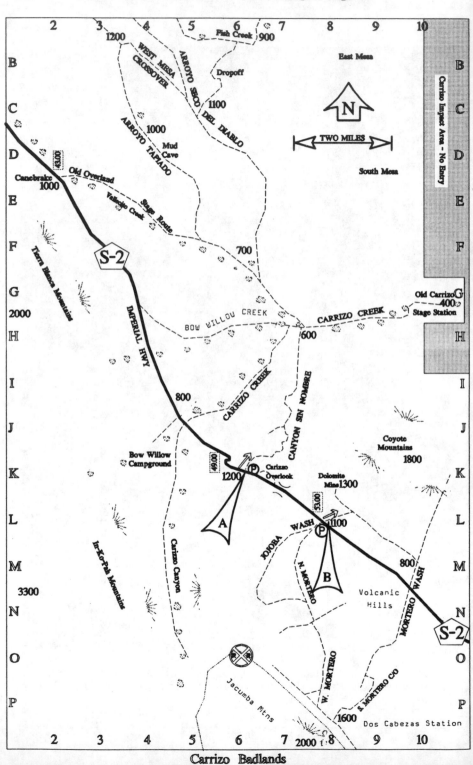

Carrizo Badlands

Tour No.:   24

Title: Carrizo Badlands and Mortero Wash Area

Overview:

The other-worldness here is awesome. The formations make one feel spooky -- spheres of natural, cemented sediments called concretions, canyons that end in "swallow holes" and caves that have collapsed forming "sinkholes", or death traps. There are caves with ceilings several stories high. These are not mountain bikable, however! In the heart of the badlands are canyons with walls dozens of feet high showing only a slit of sky above, called slot canyons. The canyon walls are of a muddy color, with little vegetation, but their textures are unbelievable. Formed by torrential erosion, columns, wrinkles and sheer vertical cliffs abound. There is a cross-over to the Fish Creek area (Tour 22) via the Diablo Dropoff. There is non-potable water in Carrizo Creek near the Carrizo Marsh and stage station site to the east. The Carrizo Impact Area beyond is closed to the public and it is regularly patrolled by park rangers.

Trip No. 24A: Canyon Sin Nombre/Carrizo Badlands

Length/Time: 26 miles; 4 hours round trip

Season: Fall through spring, cool weather only

Difficulty: Three stars

Trail Surface: Hard pack sand/dirt, 80%; dirt road, 20%

Trail Grade: Climb: 1500 feet; average grade, 2.2%

General:

Most of this trip is in canyons which have washes as floors. The sand is not usually deep and the grades are all fairly mild, but wide tires are mandatory. This tour runs within sight of most of the wonders of Carrizo Badlands and there will be plenty of people 4-wheeling on the weekends whom you may follow or seek aid from if trouble develops. The trail down Carrizo Creek to the Old Carrizo Stage Station on the east side of the area is not part of the planned round trip. However, it provides a neat detour because the Station is near running water. For this reason, it was an important Butterfield stagecoach stop. This would be a most desirable option if deep sand riding in Arroyos Tapiado and Seco del Diablo is not your bag.

Logistics:

The trip area is a two hour drive from the ocean on I-8 and lies 15 miles northwest of the town of Ocotillo on Highway S-2. When you near Mile Marker 52.0, start looking on the right for the Carrizo Badlands Overlook turnoff. You may park here, or at the trailhead which is just a short distance north of the overlook (K, 7). At any rate, park well clear of Highway S-2.

Miles from Start	Route Directions: 24A - Canyon Sin Nombre/ Carrizo Badlands	Miles to End
0.00	Head downhill northeast on Canyon Sin Nombre Trail from County Road S-2 [K,6] and pass through the gorge.	25.80
3.49	Trail merges with wash coming in from the right. [I,7]	22.31
4.07	Turn right in Carrizo Creek. [H,7] (Option: at this point you can take Carrizo Creek 3 miles to its eastern end at the old stage station site. It is interesting because in 4/10 mile, the trail becomes a 1 1/2 mile stretch of Carrizo Creek that flows year round with unusual vegetation and wildlife. This also minimizes additional sand travel. (This 6 mile detour not added to trip mileage.)	21.73
4.11	Make a sharp left turn into signed Vallecito Creek heading northwest, (notice that this is only about 200 feet from last turn!) This junction is subject to change from Flash Floods. Stop and explore carefully to select correct route. [H,7]	21.69
5.04	Take right (north) in the wide wash (Arroyo Seco del Diablo). [G,7]	20.76
10.28	Pass tributary wash on left. [C,5] No wheels!	15.52
10.86	Pass signed trail to Fish Creek via Diablo Dropoff on right. [C,5]	14.94
11.06	Pass signed Arroyo Seco del Diablo trail on right, (stay left and trail becomes the unsigned West Mesa Crossover heading northwest).	14.74
13.19	West Mesa Crossover ends in unsigned Arroyo Tapiado, turn left heading southeast. [B,3]	12.61
16.30	Big Mud Cave on left.	9.50
19.21	Merge with Vallecito Creek coming in from right. [F,5] Turn left (southeast).	6.59
21.73	Back to Carrizo Creek, turn right, west. [G/H,7]	4.07
21.78	Turn left onto Canyon Sin Nombre heading south, (the way you came in). Stop and carefully identify this junction!	4.02
24.44	Take trail to the left, (follow your tracks!). [J,7]	1.36
25.80	Back to start atop the overlook on Highway S-2.	0.00

Trip No. 24B: Mortero and Jojoba Washes Loop

Length/Time:	14 miles; three hours round trip
Season:	Fall through spring
Difficulty:	Three stars
Trail Surface:	Sandy, 60%; dirt trail, 40%
Trail Grade:	Climb: 1200 feet; average grade, 3.2%

General:
This trip is more typical of desert terrain than Trip 24A. The trip crosses Highway S-2 with the Dolomite Mine as a highlight on the north side and railroadiana highlighting the south side. Mortero Wash has a stretch or two of deep sand and some steep crossovers, but there is nothing of concern. There is one section where West Mortero Wash passes through a belt of solid volcanic rock. The abandoned railroad track and water tower at the south edge of the area are scenic remnants of days gone by.

Logistics:
Proceed northwest on Highway S-2 from I-8. Cross the Imperial/San Diego County line at Mile Marker 56. Park at signed Jojoba Wash (L,8) immediately northwest of Mile Marker 54 on Highway S-2 .

DOS CABEZAS STATION, now melting into the desert, would have seen its last revenue passenger when SD & AE through service terminated in 1951. - LL

Miles from Start	Route Directions: 24B - Mortero and Jojoba Washes Loop	Miles to End
0.0	Head northeast in Jojoba Wash from County Road S-2. (Sign says Dolomite Mine Trail). [L,8]	14.07
0.68	Turn left at fork. (Leads up to mine). [L,9]	13.39
1.46	Arrive at mine, enjoy view and return back south down same trail you came up. [K,8]	12.61
2.23	Arrive back at fork, continue straight, (stay left), to Mortero Wash. [L,9]	11.84
3.88	Turn right at intersection and head southwest (unsigned North Mortero Wash Road) [M,10]	10.19
4.56	Cross Highway S-2, continue southwest on Mortero Wash Road.	9.51
5.24	Starts to get sandy crossing Lava Flow Wash.	8.83
6.21	Enter Mortero Canyon - andesite cliffs close in.	7.86
7.18	Turn left out of Mortero Wash onto road labeled South Mortero Wash Crossover. [P,9]	6.89
7.86	High point of crossover road, railroad water tower and trestle visible. Descend into South Mortero drainage.	6.21
8.34	Post labeling South Mortero Wash, keep heading towards railroad tracks. Arrive at Dos Cabezas Station	5.73
8.44	Turn right, and head northwest on trail along abandoned railroad tracks of the SD & AE Railroad. [P,8]	5.63
8.63	Pass South Mortero Wash trestle on left.	5.44
8.92	Turn right on trail labeled West Mortero Wash. [P,7.7]	5.15
10.67	Drop down into West Mortero Wash on right. [O,8]	3.40
11.16	Canyon walls rise around you, wash gets rocky.	2.91
11.45	Rocky climb.	2.62
11.74	Steep descent. At bottom, turn right and head down wash 100 feet, then turn left on uphill trail out of wash.	2.33
12.61	Take right fork for faster exit, it really does not matter which way you take the next few intersections, the more northerly ones will take you back to start faster.	1.46
14.07	Back to start at Jojoba Wash/Highway S-2 junction.	0.00

DOS CABEZAS water tank stands its ghostly vigil over the derelict desert main line of the SD & AE railroad at mile 8.4 of Tour 24B. The happy end of the line, and story, is far to the west where the San Diego Trolley romps rejuvenated SD & AE iron. (Take your bike for a ride - call Metro Transit System 239-2644.).

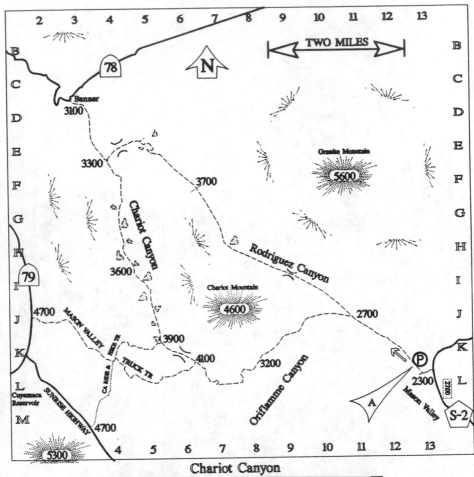

Chariot Canyon

CHARIOT CANYON gold mining district, site of the original Julian gold rush of 1870, but with renewed equipment and operations resulting from current high values of the product. - SB

Tour No.:   25

Title: Chariot Canyon

Overview:
This area is located on the mountain slopes connecting the Cuyamaca Mountains with the Anza-Borrego Desert State Park. It takes in the beauty of three canyons. Chariot Canyon is heavily dotted with riparian vegetation and gold mines. Oriflamme Canyon is a historical route used by Indians, then Spanish, Mexican, and finally, American settlers, as the easiest-direct route bridging the 3000 foot elevation difference between the mountains and desert. The occasionally rugged Rodriquez Canyon is the east leg of the loop through the area and is the least traveled of the three.

Trip No. 25A: Rodrlquez, Chariot, and Oriflamme Canyons Loop

Length/Time:	15 miles; three hours round trip
Season:	Fall through spring
Difficulty:	Four stars
Trail Surface:	Sand/dirt smooth road, 30%; moderately rocky, 60%; very rocky, 10%
Trail Grade:	Climb: 2600 feet; average grade, 6.8%

General:
This is a counter-clockwise trip through the area. There are several short steep and rocky climbs in Rodriquez Canyon, with some nice long distance views from the high point at [F,6]. A telephone line runs much of the distance through the canyon. Chariot Canyon is the most colorful leg of the trip. Through the gold mining area it is important (and posted!) that visitors stay on the road. Miners will come out of their buildings to defend their property rights if they see anyone snooping around. Much of the canyon is on state park land, which provides a place to explore off the trail. Oriflamme Canyon has dramatic vertical views, which also means that there is some serious downhill. The section between [K,5] and [K,7] is very steep and has an average 15% grade with as much as a 30% grade in spots. This unfortunately forces you to put most of your hard earned uphill pedaling into your brakes. Therefore, it would be a better downhill payback to do this area clockwise, the reverse of 25A, that is, if you don't mind walking your bike up the steep stretch of Oriflamme Canyon.

Logistics:
Take Highway 78 east out of Julian, turn right and head southeast on Highway S-2. At Mile Marker 26.8 on the west side of S-2 is a dirt road labeled "Oriflamme Canyon." Take that road about 2/10 of a mile to a fork and turn right. Park along the side of the road in this area.

Miles from Start	Route Directions: 25A - Rodriquez, Chariot, and Oriflamme Canyons Loop	Miles to End
0.0	Head northwest and up hill from the fork in the road in Mason Valley. [L,13]	14.5
1.6	Turn right into signed Rodriquez Canyon, (Oriflamme is to the left.) [J,11]	12.9
2.2	Enter state park land.	12.3
3.4	Exit state park land.	11.1
3.5	Pass small block building in small grove of trees.	11.0
4.7	Cattle guard and 4-way intersection. Stay on main trail. Start of downhill. [F,6]	9.8
5.3	Pass trail on right.	9.2
5.5	Pass trail on left.	9.0
6.3	Turn left and uphill at 3-way intersection into unsigned Chariot Canyon (right goes to Highway 78). [E,4]	8.2
6.7	Pass trail on right.	7.8
7.0	Reach high point, view of Chariot Canyon opens up.	7.5
7.1	Sign, "Entering private property, stay on road."	7.4
7.4	Golden Chariot Mine on right.	7.1
8.9	Enter state park land.	5.6
9.4	Leave the valley of Chariot Canyon, start steep uphill. (Pacific Crest Trail intersects here on the right.).	5.1
10.0	High point of trip, 3-way intersection, (stay left, Mason Valley Truck Trail to the right). Severe downhill next, (up to 30%grade).	4.5
12.2	Pass trail on right, end of killer downhill	2.3
13.0	Back to intersection of Rodriquez and Oriflamme Canyons, turn right. [J,11]	1.5
14.5	Back to start.	0.0

Appendix

Cable news: Bicyclist locks himself to tree, saves skin

NEWPORT NEWS, Va -- Mark Jones survived one of yesterday's twisters lashed to a tree.

"You couldn't breathe, man. It sucked the air right out of my lungs for about 30 seconds," said Jones, 33, a trail guide from Fort Yukon, Alaska. "It was serious."

Jones has been through Alaskan blizzards and earthquakes, but he said they don't compare to the tornado that swooped down as he bicycled his 18-speed Fuji through eastern Virginia on a cross-country trip that has already taken him 8,000 miles in six months.

Seeing the tornado behind him, Jones pulled over on a Newport News street and lashed his bike - and himself - to a tree with his bike-lock cable.

"I looked up and saw the funnel cloud. There was stuff whipping around. I wasn't about to lose a $700 mountain bike," he said. "My feet were coming up off the ground, I guarantee you that."

Jones watched the storm tear up trailers and houses nearby. And when the storm had passed, he was shaking so hard he couldn't stand.

"I sat down and, to tell you the truth, I had one beer left in my pack," Jones said, "and I drank it."

--Newport News Daily Press
in San Diego Union-Tribune
August 7, 1993

(reprinted by permission)

Table A
Factors Influencing Temperature

"Miles Inland" is included not only to give a general idea of location, but to estimate cooling as a function of ocean distance. Ambient temperature will increase approximately one degree per every two miles inland. This effect gradually fades by 20 miles inland. At that distance and beyond, "Elevation Range" has the most influence upon temperature with each 1000 feet of ascent resulting in a 2-5 degree decrease, depending on the season. Winter increases the elevation cooling effect. The "rainshadow effect" of increasing aridity and temperature commences at the mountain crests and results in the desert climate -- generally dry, temperate in winter, unforgivingly hot in summer and early fall. Telephone (619) 289-1212 for San Diego Weather Reports.

Area	Miles Inland	Elevation Range	Prime Season
COASTAL TOURS			
1. Torrey Pines, Blacks Beach	0	0-400	Spring - Fall
2. Mission Bay, Sunset Cliffs	0	0-50	All Year
3. Los Peñasquitos Canyon Preserve	4	50-500	All Year
4. San Clemente, Rose Canyon Preserve	5	75-400	All Year
5. Tecolote Canyon Preserve	5	25-400	All Year
6. Balboa Park	6	100-300	All Year
7. Otay Mesa (Dennery Canyon, or "The Pits")	7	75-500	Fall thru Spring
INLAND TOURS			
8. Lake Hodges	12	50-700	All Year
9. Mission Trails	13	250-1100	Fall thru Spring
10. Lake Poway	17	500-2300	Fall thru Spring
11. Otay Mountain	18	500-3600	Winter, Spring
12. El Capitan Reservoir	25	800-2500	Winter, Spring

Table A (Continued)
Factors Influencing Temperature

Area	Miles Inland	Elevation Range	Prime Season
MOUNTAIN TOURS			
13. Palomar Mountain	30	2000-6000	Spring, Fall
14. Indian Flats	35	2900-4400	Fall thru Spring
15. Cedar Creek	30	1000-4000	Spring thru Fall
16. Morena Reservoir	30	3000-4800	Fall thru Spring
17. Cuyamaca Mountains	35	3500-6500	All Year
18. Laguna Mountains	45	3200-6200	All Year
19. Los Coyotes Indian Res.	45	3700-5600	All Year
DESERT TOURS			
20. Coyote Canyon	50	1100-2000	Fall thru Spring
21. Grapevine Canyon	50	1400-4200	Fall thru Spring
22. Pinyon and Split Mtns.	55	300-4000	Fall thru Spring
23. Borrego Badlands	60	300-1300	Fall thru Spring
24. Carrizo Badlands	60	500-1300	Fall thru Spring
25. Chariot Canyon	50	2300-4100	Fall thru Spring

CAVEAT (L. "Let him beware")
 For desert ride planning:
   1. Carry AND drink twice as much water as you think you can.
   2. JUST SAY NO to JU, S, or T months (there's five of 'em).
   3. Equate sand and pregnancy - easy to get into, hard to get out of.

Bibliography/Recommended Reading

The following books and maps are in print (1993) and are available at major book-stores in Southern California. Contact Sunbelt Publications, telephone (619) 258-4911, for more information. These titles are recommended to enhance the understanding and enjoyment of cycling in the San Diego region.

ADVENTURING IN THE CALIFORNIA DESERT Foster 0-87156-721-0
Best single reference to the natural history and destinations in the local deserts including walks and drives in Anza-Borrego, Yuha Desert, and Salton Sea area.

AFOOT AND AFIELD IN SAN DIEGO COUNTY, 2nd Ed., Schad 0-89997-057-5
The best-selling guide to San Diego outdoors. 192 hikes are described, many are appropriate for mountain biking. Excellent maps, photos, and appendix.

ANZA-BORREGO DESERT REGION, 3rd Ed.   Lindsay   0-89997-129-6
Latest updates to the comprehensive guide to Southern California's most popular desert playground. Includes detailed map (also available separately). Details of dozens of dirt roads open to mountain bikes.

BACKCOUNTRY ROADS AND TRAILS: SAN DIEGO COUNTY Schad 0-911518-72-X
This economical book describes the natural environments and points of interest throughout America's finest county. The well-known author is a community college physical science instructor, popular outdoor guide, and lecturer.

BASIC ESSENTIALS MOUNTAIN BIKING Strassman 0-934802-47-5
One of the "Basic Essentials" series, this book covers all levels of mountain biking, from novice to pro. Safety and maintenance are also reviewed.

BICYCLE REPAIR BOOK Van der Plas 0-933201-11-7
A thorough review of bicycle maintenance, repair, and troubleshooting, covering everything from simple frame straightening to installing bicycle lights. Also useful is the guide to home-made tools and repair equipment.

BICYCLE RIDES SAN DIEGO Brundige 0-9619151-4-5
Description of bicycling trips through the valleys, canyons and mountains of San Diego County include detailed maps, difficulty, distance, and highlights.

BICYCLING THE PACIFIC COAST Kirkendall 0-89886-232-9
A detailed guidebook to the Pacific Coast bicycle route, which stretches from Mexico to Canada through California, Oregon and Washington. The 1,947 mile route is broken down into 50 mile-segments.

CALIFORNIA DESERT RECREATION MAP 1-56575-006-3
The only general utility map that shows the Salton Trough region as a whole including San Diego, Imperial, and Riverside Counties. Accurate roads, trails, and natural features are displayed.

CALIFORNIA COAST BICYCLE ROUTE-SECTION C (SANTA BARBARA TO SAN DIEGO) Bikecentennial 0-79093-269-5
This map of the southern 235 miles of the Bikecentennial Route from Santa Barbara to San Diego, includes a listing of campgrounds, hostels, route conditions, bike shops, scenic and cultural attractions.

CALIFORNIA OHV GUIDEBOOK Llewellyn 0-941925-10-2
Complete guidebook to off-highway vehicular recreation in California. Includes maps and other information about OHV areas and "green sticker roads." With index and locator maps, this book is both highly informative and easy to use - a "must" for every OHV enthusiast who wants to go adventuring beyond the pavement's end. Many trails suitable for mountain biking.

CUYAMACA RANCHO STATE PARK HIKE MAP Harrison 1-877689-05-X
A detailed map of Cuyamaca Rancho State Park showing campgrounds, hiking and horseback riding trails, and topography. Mountain bike routes are clearly delineated.

CYCLING SAN DIEGO, 2nd Ed., Schad 0-961728-83-3
Newly revised, comprehensive guide to 60 day trips in San Diego County ranging from leisurely rides to more difficult routes including cultural and natural features.

MOUNTAIN BICYCLING SAN GABRIELS Immler 0-89997-078-8
Includes over 30 tours in the Los Angeles National Forest, ranging in length from 2 to 35 miles, and varying in difficulty from easy to rides up mountain peaks. Distance and elevation gain are included with each description.

MOUNTAIN BIKE BOOK Van der Plas 0-933201-18-4
A concise, but thorough guide suitable for both beginning and experienced riders. Selecting and equipping the bike, safe off-road riding and handling skills, and maintenance are all discussed.

MOUNTAIN BIKE CALIFORNIA #7 SANTA MONICAS Hosenover 0-938665-10-3
This newly revised guide describes routes in the Santa Monica Mountains National Recreation Area. Nearly 59 rides from the Hollywood Hills to Pt. Mugu State Park are include along with maps and parking information.

MOUNTAIN BIKE CALIFORNIA #8 ANGELES NATIONAL FOREST Troy 0-938665-09-X
One of a series - mountain biking the Coast Ranges. This guide includes the Saugus district of the Angeles National Forest with Mt. Pinos including a natural history of the Saugus district.

MOUNTAIN BIKE CALIFORNIA #9 SAN GABRIEL MOUNTAINS Troy 0-938665-11-1 The latest trail information in the Angeles National Forest and San Gabriel Mountains is available in this book. 12 detailed maps are included.

MOUNTAIN BIKE REPAIR HANDBOOK Coello 1-55821-064-4
With their novel design, equipment, and rugged use, mountain bikes take some
special knowledge for continual smooth, trouble-free operation. Author Coello
covers all areas of repair and maintenance.

MOUNTAIN BIKING AROUND LOS ANGELES Immler 0-89997-109-1
Listed are 32 mountain bicycling trips in the grater Los Angeles area, form
Malibu to Orange County. Total distance, difficult, elevation gain or loss, time
to complete the trip, and a map is included for each trip.

MOUNTAIN BIKING SOUTHERN CALIFORNIA'S BEST 100 TRAILS
Douglass and Fragnoli 0-938665-20-0
All the best places to ride a mountain bike--from San Diego to San Luis Obispo,
from the Sierra Nevada to Death Valley and the Mojave Desert--the west's
leading mountain biking authors share their top choices of fat-tired routes.

SAN DIEGO: INTRODUCTION TO REGION 3rd Ed. Pryde 0-8403-3233-5
THE reference to the natural environments of the county. Includes: Geology,
Climate, Soils, Vegetation, Wildlife, Water Supply (most important!).

SAN DIEGO BACKCOUNTRY REC. MAP Harrison 1-877689-00-9
A superb full color map for outdoor enthusiasts and naturalists who need East
County's mountains and deserts on one handy and frequently updated map.:
Features topographic information, water features, roads and trails, campsites.

SAN DIEGO COUNTY, AAA GUIDEBOOK
From Mission Bay to Borrego Springs, from Coronado to Lake Cuyamaca, San
Diego County encompasses beaches, canyons, mountains and desert. This latest
Auto Club 300-plus-page San Diego County guidebook contains more than 140
photographs and 30 maps, all in full color.

SIDEKICK MAP-COYOTE CANYON Sidekick 1-880824-06-X
Map and textual guide to off-road trails in Coyote Canyon north of Borrego
Springs. Trails are rated, and the accompanying text describes routes and off-
road riding tips. Also good for mountain biking and hiking.

SIDEKICK MAP-LOS COYOTES/WARNER Sidekick 1-88024-03-5
A map and accompanying text for off-road trails in the Warner Springs/Los
Coyotes Indian Reservation area. Trail routes are rated on difficulty. The text
offers various tips. Useful for mountain biking.

SIDEKICK MAP-SMUGGLER'S CAVE Sidekick 1-880824-16-7
Located 65 miles east of San Diego off Highway 8 near the town of Jacumba.
Explore a cave used by smugglers in the 1800's, a section of the Butterfield
Overland Stage route or enjoy the vistas of the old railroad.

WEEKENDERS GUIDE: ANZA-BORREGO 2nd Ed.Johnson   0-910805-05-9
Rides along paved and dirt desert roads with all-color photos by a veteran Anza-
Borrego naturalist and professional photographer. Detailed maps supplement
descriptions with post mile markers carefully locating points of interest.

Index

Author Profile

Scott Bringe is a native San Diegan who at a very early age decried the use of training wheels on his low-boy bike. Much to his mother's horror and his father's amazement, he first made the trip down the family driveway, through the cactus garden and over the curb (sans training wheels) - without falling off! Scott has been biking the unusual ever since. A photojournalism graduate of the Walter Cronkite School of Journalism at Arizona State University, Scott has urned his outdoor adventure hobbies into a career. With three books and veral magazine articles to his credit, he still finds time to develop surfboards r stationary surfing in river whitewater and to pursue desert preservation iects in the Valley of the Sun from his namesake base in Scottsdale, Arizona.